A FRENCH VOCABULARY FOR ADVANCED LEVEL

By the same author

A FRENCH VOCABULARY FOR ORDINARY LEVEL
72 pp., limp.

A FRENCH VOCABULARY FOR ADVANCED LEVEL

BY

I. C. THIMANN, B.A., B.Com., Ph.D.

Chief Modern Language Master
Nottingham High School

HARRAP LONDON

First published in Great Britain 1963
by GEORGE G. HARRAP & CO. LTD
182 High Holborn, London WC1V 7AX

Reprinted: 1964; 1965; 1966; 1968; 1970; 1972; 1973
Reprinted with corrections: 1974
Reprinted: 1976 (*twice*); 1977; 1978; 1979 (*twice*);
1980

ISBN 0 245 56140 4

Printed in Great Britain by
Biddles Ltd, Guildford, Surrey

FOREWORD

THE transition from Ordinary Level French Essays to those of the Advanced Level is a difficult one. The pupil of sixteen or so who has 'written up' stories from a plan, or from a set of pictures, or who has merely reproduced anecdotes read to him, is in very difficult country when asked to produce three hundred and fifty words on a subject such as *L'Influence de la Télévision* or *Ma Maison idéale*—let alone on an abstract topic.

I believe that the Advanced Level candidate will be greatly assisted if, during his two or three years in a Sixth Form, he has written essays on some of the topics in this book, using the extensive vocabularies and phrases provided. Most of the topics have been suggested by the essay subjects set by the various Examining Boards during the last few years.

Some teachers build up a Free Composition by oral methods—*i.e.*, by constructing the nexus of an essay as a result of question and answer. Others favour the study or learning of passages in French on the same theme which can, by fair means or foul, be introduced into an essay: thus a passage from *Vol de Nuit* or *Pêcheur d'Islande* may be read before beginning a composition that centres on Aviation or the Sea. Yet neither of these methods affords that practice in *improvisation* so necessary to the examinee. It is probable that, under examination conditions, the candidate will have to make an entirely new plan; and the special vocabularies which he has learned will be the only straw at which he can clutch.

One possible advantage of the present book is that, as a result of reading a large number of current books and periodicals, I have been able to supply a vocabulary that is rather more up to date than that of the average dictionary or Sixth Form course. The Advanced Level Essay topic is slowly moving from the familiar themes of the past, such as Hiking and Railways, to Science, Television, and Space Travel, and the requisite words are, as a rule, not at the Sixth-Former's disposal.

As far as is possible, nouns are grouped together under various headings; verbs and adjectives, as well as nouns, are given, as are the relevant phrases or idioms. Indications are also given of the difference between the various French words recorded as the equivalents of an English one. It is unhelpful, to put it mildly, to write: time-table—*un horaire*, *un indicateur*. Unexplained French equivalents may, indeed, do the student more harm than good, and will certainly aggravate the task of the marker.

For abstract topics, such as the well-worn *La Fin justifie les Moyens*, it is practically impossible to give special vocabularies, but the list of phrases suited to reasoned or reflective writing should prove useful.

Every Sixth-Form teacher is constantly urging his pupils not only to make an essay plan *before* writing but to re-read *after* writing, in order to eliminate minor slips and grammatical errors. The candidate himself should see to it that his language is reasonably varied, and if he will study the section entitled

'Enrich your French!' (p. 93 *ff.*) he should go some way towards attaining this end.

To keep this work as slight as possible, I have avoided all the simpler words and expressions that a candidate ought to know on entering the Sixth Form—they may, in any case, be found in Harrap's *A French Vocabulary for Ordinary Level.* The same word, however, may well appear in different sections of the present work—*e.g.*, *l'écran* under the subject heading of Cinema, War, and Television.

Finally, as there is, for purposes of vocabulary, no water-tight compartment between Free Composition and Translation into French, this book should provide useful material for the latter activity.

I.C.T.

CONTENTS

1. WORD AND PHRASE LISTS AND ESSAY TOPICS

Subjects

1. WORD AND PHRASE LISTS AND ESSAY TOPICS

1. ARCHITECTURE—L'ARCHITECTURE (*f.*)

Cathedral or Church

column	**la colonne**	stained-glass window	**le vitrail** (*pl.* **les vitraux**)
pillar	**le pilier**	altar	**un autel**
capital	**le chapiteau**	rose window	**la rosace**
vault (*of ceiling*)	**la voûte**	belfry	**le clocher**
Roman (Norman) arch	**l'arc en plein-cintre**	nave	**la nef**
Gothic arch	**l'arc en ogive**	aisle	**le bas-côté**
base	**le socle**	choir	**le chœur**
flying buttress	**un arc-boutant**	transept	**le transept**
doorway	**le portail**	clerestory	**la claire-voie**
gargoyle	**la gargouille**	organ	**un orgue**
spire	**la flèche**	cemetery	**le cimetière**
tower	**la tour**	tomb	**la tombe** (grave); **le tombeau** (gravestone)
apse	**une abside**		
pulpit	**la chaire**		

Castle

turret	**la tourelle**	keep	**le donjon**
wall	**la muraille** (*for defence*)	loophole	**la meurtrière**
drawbridge	**le pont-levis**	moat	**le fossé**

Sections of Building

front	**la façade**	first storey	**le premier étage**
rear	**le derrière**	area	**la superficie**
view	**la perspective**	height	**la hauteur**
ground floor	**le rez-de-chaussée**		

People

architect	**un architecte**	mason	**le maçon**
sculptor	**le sculpteur**		

Public Building

hospital	**un hôpital**	block of flats	**un immeuble**
public library	**la bibliothèque**	museum	**le musée**
town hall	**l'Hôtel de Ville** (*m.*)		

Adjectives

shaded (by)	**ombragé (de)**	ugly	**laid, hideux**
topped (by)	**surmonté (de)**	imposing	**imposant**
majestic	**majestueux**	graceful	**gracieux**
deplorable	**lamentable**	spacious	**spacieux**

Verbs

to contain	**renfermer**	to demolish	**démolir**
to loom up, rise up	**se dresser**	to commemorate	**commémorer**
		to project	**faire saillir**
to tower above	**dominer**	to look out on	**donner sur**
to erect	**ériger**	to draw up (a plan)	**dresser (un plan)**
to set off	**rehausser, mettre en relief**	to be suited to	**convenir à**

Idioms

to be out of proportion	**être mal proportionné**
you get to it by . . .	**on y accède par...**
a building in execrable taste	**un bâtiment d'un goût détestable**
the park adjoins it	**le parc y fait suite**
to cover an area of . . .	**s'étendre sur une superficie de...**
to date from the 17th century	**dater du (remonter au) dix-septième siècle**
one of the finest buildings as regards height	**un des plus beaux bâtiments quant à la hauteur**
to come into view	**s'offrir aux regards**
to be hemmed in by the surrounding buildings	**être étouffé par les bâtiments voisins**
a relic of past glories	**un vestige d'une gloire disparue**
to look like a prison	**présenter l'aspect d'une prison**
to look out of place	**avoir l'air déplacé**

ESSAYS

Description d'une cathédrale (d'une église).
Le plus beau bâtiment de ma ville (*or*, que je connaisse).
Les impressions que vous inspire la visite d'un château historique.

See also 37. TOWN.

2. ARMY—L'ARMÉE (*f.*)

Ranks

rank	**le grade**	major	**le commandant**
private	**le simple soldat**	brigadier-general	**le général de brigade**
N.C.O.	**le sous-officier**		
corporal (*infantry*)	**le caporal**	lieutenant-general	**le général de division**
sergeant	**le sergent**		
sergeant-major	**un adjudant**	general	**le général d'armée**
second-lieutenant	**le sous-lieutenant**	field-marshal	**le maréchal**
captain	**le capitaine**		

People

guard	**le garde**
conscript	**le conscrit**
recruit	**la recrue**
sentry	**la sentinelle**
orderly	**le planton**
infantryman	**le fantassin**
civilian (*e.g.*, clerk)	**le civil**
retired officer	**un officier retraité**
war correspondent	**le correspondant de guerre, aux armèes**
spy	**un espion**
War Minister	**le Ministre de la Guerre**

Branches of Army

staff	**l'état-major (*m.*)**
service corps	**le train des équipages**
engineers	**le génie**
artillery	**l'artillerie (*f.*)**
commando troops	**les commandos (*m.*)**
ordnance	**le service du matèriel**
airborne troops	**les troupes aéroportées**
infantry	**l'infanterie (*f.*)**
signals	**le corps des transmissions, les transmissions (*f.*)**
A.A. defence	**la défense contre avions (D.C.A.)**
army of occupation	**une armée d'occupation**
military band	**la musique militaire**
standing army	**l'armée permanente**

Weapons and Transport

weapon	**une arme**
shell	**un obus**
rocket	**la fusée**
A.A. gun	**le canon anti-aérien**
A.A. battery	**la batterie de défense anti-aérienne**
tank	**le char (de combat), le tank**
missile	**le projectile**
bullet	**la balle**
explosive	**un explosif**
flame-thrower	**le lance-flammes**
hand grenade	**la grenade à main**
armoured car	**la voiture blindée, l'auto-mitrailleuse (*f.*)**
jeep	**la jeep**
machine-gun	**la mitrailleuse**
tommy-gun	**la mitraillette**
bayonet	**la baïonnette**
cannon-ball	**le boulet**
caterpillar	**un engin chenillé**

Defences

barbed wire	**les barbelés (*m.*)**
trench	**la tranchée**
minefield	**le champ de mines**

Groups

squad	**une escouade**
patrol	**la patrouille**
platoon	**le peloton**
battalion	**le bataillon**
regiment	**le régiment**
unit	**une unité**
reinforcements	**les renforts (*m.*)**
troops	**les troupes (*f.*)**
guerrillas	**les guérilleros (*m.*)**

Places, Buildings, Sectors

barracks	**la caserne**	base	**le point d'appui**
sentry box	**la guérite**	mess	**le mess**
front	**le front**		

Minor Equipment and Comforts

uniform	**un uniforme**	pay	**la solde**
water bottle	**le bidon**	leave	**le congé; la permission** (*shorter*)
grub	**le rata, la mangeaille, la boustifaille**		

Forms of Fighting

siege	**le siège**	set-back	**un échec**
local engagements	**les actions locales**	street fighting	**les combats** (*m.*) **de rue**
guerrilla warfare	**la guérilla**	thrust	**la poussée**
tactics	**la tactique**	bridgehead	**la tête de front**
blockade	**le blocus**	offensive	**une offensive**
reprisals	**les représailles** (*f.*)		

Truce

truce	**la trêve**	surrender	**la reddition**
armistice	**un armistice**	war-weariness	**la lassitude de la guerre**
cease-fire	**le cessez-le-feu**		

Functions

Field Day	**le Jour des (la Journée de) Manœuvres**	medical inspection	**la visite médicale**
		eyesight test	**un examen visuel**

Damage

damage	**les dommages** (*m.*), **les dégâts** (*m.*)	wound	**la blessure; la plaie** (*open*)
		scar	**la cicatrice**
loss	**la perte**		

Orders

halt!	**halte!**	present arms!	**présentez armes!**
quick march!	**en avant, marche!**	attention!	**garde à vous!**
		shoulder arms!	**en joue!**
stand at ease!	**repos!**	fire!	**feu!**

Adjectives

brave	**courageux**	cowardly	**lâche**
bold	**hardi, intrépide**	mechanised	**mécanisé**
tough	**dur**		

Verbs

to aim at	viser	to patrol	patrouiller
to fire (at)	tirer (sur)	to grouse	rouspéter
to invade	envahir	to call up, call to the colours	appeler au service, sous les drapeaux (*m.*)
to fall back on	refluer sur, se replier sur	to hit (*of bullets*)	toucher
to shoot (dead)	fusiller	to win (victories)	remporter (des victoires, *f.*)
to camouflage	camoufler	to put down (a revolt)	réprimer (une révolte)
to fight (a battle)	livrer (bataille)	to review	passer en revue
to inflict (losses)	infliger (des pertes)	to encircle	encercler, cerner
to flee	fuir, prendre la fuite	to police	maintenir l'ordre
to lay down (arms)	mettre bas (les armes)	to crackle (*of gunfire*)	crépiter
to parade (*intrans.*)	se rassembler		
to bark out (orders)	brailler (des commandements)		

Phrases

to answer the call-up	répondre à l'appel
to be unfit for service	être inapte au service
to see the world	voir du pays, voir un peu le monde
to stand to attention	se mettre au garde à vous
he was given 10 days' cells	on lui flanqua dix jours de tôle (salle de police)
to troop the colours	faire la présentation du drapeau
to have a decorative role	avoir un rôle décoratif
to attain one's objective	atteindre son objectif
to remain on conquered territory	rester en territoire conquis
to be short of ammunition	être à court de munitions
to come back safe and sound	revenir intact (indemne)
with fixed bayonet	(la) baïonnette au canon
to fire at long range	tirer à longue portée
to hold at bay, in check	tenir en échec
to rise from the ranks	sortir du rang

ESSAYS

Une carrière dans l'armée.
L'entraînement militaire dans les écoles (la C.C.F.): est-ce une perte de temps?
Une bataille historique.
Le rôle de l'armée dans le monde moderne.
Les avantages et les inconvénients du service militaire obligatoire.
Le métier de soldat.

See also 38. WAR.

3. AVIATION—L'AVIATION (*f.*)

Military Personnel

airman	un aviateur	observer	un observateur
mechanic	le mécanicien	wireless operator	le radio
navigator	le navigateur	Fleet Air Arm	l'Aéronavale (*f.*)

Planes

monoplane	le monoplan	pilotless aircraft	un avion sans pilote
biplane	le biplan	wreck	une épave
four-engined plane	le quadrimoteur	helicopter	un hélicoptère
fighter	un avion de chasse	flight	une escadrille
bomber	le bombardier	squadron	un escadron
jet	un avion à réaction	balloon	le ballon
plane with fold-back wings	un avion à ailes repliables	airship	le dirigeable

Raids

raid	le raid, une attaque	bomb	la bombe
dive-bombing attack	le piqué, le bombardement en piqué	rocket	la fusée
shelter	un abri	direct hit	le coup direct
target	la cible	flak	le tir contre-avions
		bomb sight	le viseur
		bomb crater	un entonnoir

Functions, Tasks

fly-past	le défilé aérien	landing	l'atterrissage (*m.*)
air display	le festival aérien, la fête aéronautique	take-off	le décollage, l'envol (*m.*)
aerobatics	l'acrobatie (*f.*)	trial flight	le vol d'essai
upkeep, maintenance	l'entretien (*m.*)		

Civil Personnel

pilot	le pilote	crew	un équipage
co-pilot	le co-pilote	test pilot	le pilote d'essai
air hostess	l'hôtesse de l'air	dare-devil	le casse-cou

Airport

airport	un aéroport	control tower	la tour de contrôle
air terminal	une aérogare	gangway	la passerelle
airfield	le champ d'aviation	petrol tanker	le camion d'essence
hangar	le hangar		
landing strip	la piste d'atterrissage; la piste d'envol (*for take-off*)		

Gliding

glider	le planeur	cable	le câble
gliding	le vol à voiles	to tow	remorquer
gliding fan	le vélivole	to let go	lâcher
launching	le lâcher	to pay out	déhaler
winch	le treuil	to land	se poser

General Parts of Plane

wing-tip	un aileron	lever	la manette
tail (-unit)	l'empennage (*m.*)	joystick	le manche à balai
wing span	l'envergure (*f.*)		
cockpit	un habitacle, la carlingue	porthole	le hublot
		gangway (between seats)	le couloir
undercarriage	le train d'atterrissage	safety belt	la ceinture de sécurité
pressurised cabin	la cabine étanche		
propeller	une hélice	parachute	le parachute

Jets

turbo-jet (engine)	le turbo-réacteur	nozzle	la tuyère
exhaust	l'échappement (*m.*)		

Verbs

to land	atterrir	to refuel	ravitailler
to take off	s'envoler, décoller	to misfire, cut out	avoir des ratés, bafouiller
to come down on the sea	amerrir	to taxi	rouler
to fly over	survoler	to repair	dépanner
to crash	s'écraser	to consume (petrol)	consommer (l'essence)
to shoot down	abattre		
to locate	repérer	to call at	faire escale à
to turn, bank	virer	to fly (a plane)	piloter (un avion)
to throb (*of engines*)	ronfler, vrombir		

Phrases

to travel by air	voyager par avion
to be airsick	avoir le mal de l'air
to break the sound barrier	franchir le mur du son
to reach the speed of sound	atteindre la vitesse du son
to make a forced landing	faire un atterrissage forcé
to be at the controls	être aux commandes
to hedge-hop	faire du rase-mottes
to check one's route via the compass	corriger sa route à la boussole
to make height	prendre de la hauteur
in bad visibility	par mauvaise visibilité
to return after carrying out one's mission	revenir mission accomplie
to make a dive-bombing attack	attaquer en piqué
to loop the loop	boucler la boucle
it's a piece of cake!	c'est du gâteau!
he has had 100 hours' flying	il a totalisé cent heures de vol
to have air supremacy	avoir la maîtrise de l'air
there remained nothing of the plane but scattered wreckage and burned bodies	de l'avion il ne restait que quelques débris épars et des corps carbonisés
wreckage scattered over a wide area	des débris éparpillés sur une grande étendue

ESSAYS

Un combat aérien.
L'avenir du transport aérien.
Une visite à un aérodrome.
Un accident d'avion.
Londres-New York. Avion ou paquebot?
Le rôle des armées aériennes.

4. CINEMA—LE CINÉMA

Cinema, Film Studio

house	**la salle**	news cinema	**le cinéma d'actualités (cin'act)**
seat	**la place**		
ticket	**le billet**		
desk	**le guichet**	continuous performance	**la séance permanente**
torch	**la lampe électrique**	performance, show	**la séance**
screen	**un écran**	studio	**le studio**
gangway	**le couloir**	movie camera	**la caméra**
way out	**la sortie**	arc lamp	**la lampe à arc**

Films

science-fiction film	**le film d'anticipation**	supporting film	**le film supplémentaire**
advertisement film	**le film publicitaire**	thriller	**le film à sensation**
horror film	**le film d'horreur**	trailer	**le film annonce**
sound film (talkie)	**le film sonore (parlant)**	short	**le court métrage**
		sound track	**la bande sonore**
silent film	**le film muet**	revival	**la reprise**
crime film	**le film policier**	credit titles	**le générique**
newsreel	**les actualités (*f.*)**	sub-title	**le sous-titre**
cartoon	**le dessin animé**	sequence	**la séquence**
Western	**le Western**		
documentary	**le film documentaire**		

People

star	**la vedette, la star**	producer	**le réalisateur**
Hollywood magnate	**le magnat de Hollywood**	director	**le metteur en scène**
script-writer	**le, la, scénariste**	starlet	**la starlette**
usherette	**une ouvreuse**	extra	**un(e) figurant(e)**
double, understudy	**la doublure**	film fan, cinema-goer	**le cinéphile**
stand-in	**un(e) remplaçant(e)**	operator	**un opérateur**

Adjectives

feeble	**banal**	moving	**émouvant**
thrilling	**passionnant, palpitant**	outstanding	**saillant**

Verbs

to frequent	**fréquenter**	to be a flop	**être un four**
to shoot	**tourner**	to sign up (a star)	**engager (une vedette)**
to film (a novel)	**filmer (un roman), mettre en scène (un roman)**	to dub (in English)	**doubler (en anglais)**
to understudy (a part)	**doubler (un rôle)**	to make up	**maquiller**
		to be popular	**être en vogue**

Phrases

this film is coming to our cinema	**ce film passera dans notre cinéma**
a film not to be missed	**un film à ne pas manquer**
she put up a delightful performance	**elle a joué à ravir**
children under 16 not admitted	**interdit aux moins de seize ans**
it's the highlight of the programme	**c'est le clou du programme**
this film has had a resounding success	**ce film a eu un succès retentissant**
in slow motion	**en ralenti**
I don't think much of the plot	**l'intrigue ne me dit pas grand'chose**
I'm surprised the film got past the censor	**je m'étonne que le film ait été approuvé par la censure**
the cinema is within everybody's means	**le cinéma est à la portée de toutes les bourses**
the hooligans in the back row spoiled my pleasure	**les voyous du dernier rang ont gâté mon plaisir**
it's running at the Plaza	**il se joue au Plaza**
this film made a packet in the U.S.A.	**ce film a fait d'énormes recettes aux États-Unis**
the film sticks closely to the novel	**le film ne s'écarte pas du roman**
the suspense was intolerable	**le suspense était insupportable**

ESSAYS

Une visite au cinéma.
Le cinéma est-il en déclin?
Le cinéma: art ou industrie?
Un film que j'ai vu.
La vie et la mort d'une vedette de cinéma.
Le cinéma et la délinquance juvénile.
Le cinéma devant la menace de la télévision.

See also 36. THEATRE.

5. THE CIRCUS—LE CIRQUE

People

travelling showman	**le forain**	funny man	**le comique**
travelling circus	**le cirque ambulant**	tightrope-walker	**le funambule**
		rider	**un écuyer, une écuyère**
acrobat	**un(e) acrobate**		
clown	**le clown**	star	**une étoile**
tamer	**le dompteur**	trapeze artist	**le, la, trapéziste**
M.C.	**le maître de manège**		

Animals

pony	**le poney**	troop of lions	**la troupe des lions**
sea-lion	**une otarie**		
chimpanzee	**le chimpanzé**		

Turns

act	**un acte**	the high spot	**le point culminant, le clou**
elephants' ballet	**le ballet d'éléphants**		
equestrian number	**un numéro équestre**	trick-riding act	**un numéro de voltige**
acrobatics	**les acrobaties (*f.*)**		

Apparatus

arc-lamp	**la lampe à arc**	sawdust	**la sciure**
net	**le filet**		

Parts of Circus

arena	**une arène**	Big Top	**le grand chapiteau**
bar (of a cage)	**le barreau (d'une cage)**	track, ring	**la piste**

Adjectives

breathless, in suspense	**haletant, en suspens**

Verbs

to hold one's breath	**retenir son souffle**	to rehearse	**répéter**

Phrases

to balance a barrel on the top of your nose	**tenir un baril en équilibre sur le bout du nez**
the lion-tamer cracks his whip	**le dompteur de lions fait claquer son fouet**
to jump through the hoop to the accompaniment of a drum roll	**sauter à travers le cerceau à l'accompagnement d'un roulement de tambour**
to stand on tip-toe	**se tenir sur la pointe des pieds**
to flirt with death	**jouer avec la mort**
to execute a solo number	exécuter un numéro en solo
he was hanging by his feet from the trapeze	**il était suspendu au trapèze par les pieds**
to project a man from a gun	**lancer un homme par un canon**
they look positively human!	**ils semblent presque humains!**
they do some amazing tricks	**ils réussissent des tours extraordinaires**
to go through a rigorous training	**subir un dur entraînement**
the audience couldn't believe its eyes	**le public ne pouvait en croire ses yeux**
to display remarkable skill	**faire preuve d'une adresse remarquable**
at a dizzy height	**à une hauteur vertigineuse**

ESSAY

Une visite au Cirque.

6. COMMERCE—LE COMMERCE

Banks

bank account	le compte en banque	safe	le coffre-fort
cashier	le caissier	cheque-book	le carnet de chèques
bank manager	le directeur de banque	to cash a cheque	encaisser un chèque
bank clerk	l'employé(e) de banque	to make out a cheque	faire un chèque

Office

boss	le gérant	carbon paper	le (papier) carbone
shorthand-typist	la sténo-dactylo	to answer the telephone	répondre au téléphone
secretary	le (la) secrétaire	to type	taper à la machine
telephonist	le (la) téléphoniste	to cyclostyle	polycopier
staff	le personnel	to go through the mail	dépouiller le courrier
switchboard	le standard		
typewriter	la machine à écrire		

Market

seller	le vendeur (la vendeuse)	wares (foodstuffs)	les denrées (*f.*)
housewife	la ménagère	goods	les marchandises (*f.*)
stall	un étalage	change	la (petite) monnaie
range (of goods)	la gamme		

Shop

branch, chain-store	la succursale	night watchman	le gardien de nuit
departmental stores	les grands magasins	clients	la clientèle
tradesman	le commerçant	lift	un ascenseur
wholesaler	le marchand en gros, le grossiste	moving staircase	un escalier roulant
retailer	le détaillant	counter	le comptoir
shop assistant	le commis; le vendeur, (la vendeuse)	show-case	la vitrine
shop-lifter	le voleur (la voleuse) à l'étalage	shop front	la devanture
partner	un associé	warehouse	un entrepôt
middleman	un intermédiaire	purchase	une emplette, un achat
supplier	le fournisseur	till	le tiroir-caisse
consumer	le consommateur	order	la commande
commercial traveller	le commis, le voyageur de commerce	increase (*in prices*)	la hausse, la majoration
		reduction (*in prices*)	la baisse

Companies

firm	la maison de commerce, la firme	interest	l'intérêt (*m.*)
assets	l'actif (*m.*)	dividend	le dividende
liabilities	le passif	shareholder	un(e) actionnaire
profit	le bénéfice	stockbroker	un agent de change
loss	la perte	Stock Exchange	la Bourse
accountant	le comptable	share	une action
business tycoon	le magnat	expenses	les frais (*m.*)
capital	le capital	to go bankrupt	faire faillite

Money

pound	la livre sterling	cost of living	le coût de la vie
paper money	le papier-monnaie	high cost of living	la vie chère
coin	la pièce	tax	un impôt
note	le billet	taxation	la taxation
exchange rate	le taux	taxpayer	le contribuable
foreign currency	les devises (étrangères)	subsidy	la subvention
purchasing power	le pouvoir d'achat	budget	le budget
		rent	le loyer
		wages	le salaire

Adjective

competitive (*price*)	compétitif

Verbs (general)

to dismiss	congédier	to wrap up, pack	emballer
to despatch	expédier	to buy second-hand	acheter d'occasion
to order	commander	to afford	se permettre, avoir les moyens de
to take on (*staff*)	engager	to charge	demander
to invest	placer	to save	faire des économies
to display	étaler	to balance (*budget*)	équilibrer
to put up (*prices*)	augmenter, majorer		
to reduce (*prices*)	baisser, réduire		
to bid	faire une offre		
to outbid	renchérir sur		
to cover (expenses)	couvrir (les frais)		

Phrases

to sell for cash (on credit; wholesale; retail)	vendre au comptant (à crédit; en gros; au détail)
to put onto the market	lancer sur le marché
to do well, to do good business	faire de bonnes affaires
it cost him a packet	ça lui a coûté des sommes folles
I can't make ends meet	je n'arrive pas à joindre les deux bouts
to have a deficit of £10,000	être en déficit de dix mille livres
to pay high interest charges	payer de gros intérêts
the staff consists of . . .	le personnel comprend...
they bang the door in your face	ils vous ferment la porte au nez
to go from door to door	faire du porte à porte

to make eyes at the boss	**faire de l'œil au patron**
to earn £2000 p.a. with expenses	**gagner £2000 par an, plus les frais**
we've only a small staff	**nous n'avons qu'un personnel restreint**
to make substantial economies	**procéder à de sérieuses compressions**
it's a pretty dull routine	**c'est une routine fort monotone**
to act on one's own initiative	**prendre des initiatives**
to deliver to the door	**livrer à domicile**
to make a good bargain	**faire une bonne affaire**
to go shopping	**faire ses courses**
to earn one's living	**gagner son pain**
'Would there be anything else?'	**'Et avec ça?'**
to be hard up	**être dans la gêne, être à court d'argent**
what a crowd!	**que de monde!**
to go window-gazing (window-shopping)	**faire du lèche-vitrines**

ESSAYS

Les avantages et les désavantages de la vente à tempérament (hire purchase).
Une vente aux enchères (auction sale).
La journée d'un commis-voyageur.
L'argent.
Une visite au marché.
Une aventure dans un grand magasin.
La vie d'une sténo-dactylo *ou* d'un employé de banque: quel triste métier!

7. THE COUNTRYSIDE—LA CAMPAGNE

Features

heath, moor	**la bruyère, la lande**	windmill	**le moulin à vent**
		watermill	**le moulin à eau**
copse	**le taillis**	ditch	**le fossé**
marsh	**le marais**	thicket	**le fourré**
hedge	**la haie**	brushwood	**la broussaille**
slope	**le talus, la pente**	bough	**le rameau**
path	**le sentier**	spring	**la source**
pond	**la mare, un étang**	valley	**la vallée**

Village

village	**le village**	village green	**la place du village**
hamlet	**le hameau**	village store	**l'épicerie (*f.*) du village**
inn	**une auberge**		

Homes

cottage	**la chaumière**	country house	**le château, la maison de campagne**
hut	**la cabane**		

People

countryman	**le campagnard, le paysan**	yokel	**le rustre**
		village policeman	**le garde champêtre**
country folk	**les ruraux (*m.*)**		

Extent of Country

countryside	**la région**	region (*geographical*)	**une contrée**

Pleasures

attractions	**les charmes** (*m.*)	absence of noise	**l'absence** (*f.*) **de bruit**
fresh air	**l'air frais**		
smell of hay	**l'odeur** (*f.*) **des foins** (*m.*)	absence of smoke	**l'absence de fumée**
smell of wet earth	**l'odeur de la terre mouillée**	healthy diet	**un régime sain (salubre)**
quietness	**la paix**		

Flowers

buttercup	**le bouton d'or**	cowslip	**le coucou**
daisy	**la pâquerette**	poppy	**le coquelicot**
dandelion	**le pissenlit**		

Disadvantages

smell of manure	**l'odeur** (*f.*) **du fumier**	loneliness	**l'isolement** (*m.*)
		distance from shops	**l'éloignement** (*m.*) **des magasins**
mud	**la boue**		
puddle	**la flaque**		
pot-hole, rut	**une ornière, la fondrière**	monotony	**la monotonie**
		boredom	**l'ennui** (*m.*)
pylon	**le pylône électrique**	bad weather	**les intempéries** (*f.*)

Adjectives

muddy	**boueux**	healthy	**hygiénique, salubre, sain**
marshy	**marécageux**		
uneven	**raboteux**	wild	**sauvage**
picturesque	**pittoresque**	insanitary	**insalubre**
wooded	**boisé**		

Verbs

to wind (*of path*)	**serpenter**	to inhale	**humer**

Phrases

in the open country	**en rase campagne**
to stretch as far as the eye can see	**s'étendre à perte de vue**
to sleep in the open air	**coucher à la belle étoile**
to live close to nature	**vivre près de la nature**
to breathe deeply	**respirer à pleins poumons**
to go across country	**prendre à travers champs**
in the fresh air	**en plein air**

to get some exercise	**prendre de l'exercice**
paths fragrant with honeysuckle	**des chemins qui embaument le chèvrefeuille**
the roads become rivers of mud	**les chemins se transforment en ruisseaux de boue**
to go into town every day	**aller à la ville tous les jours**
to get away from the hectic life of the town	**échapper à la vie fiévreuse de la ville**
to have the best of both worlds	**avoir les avantages de l'un et de l'autre**
to eat lots of good food	**manger abondamment une nourriture saine**
that's its worst defect	**c'est là son pire défaut**

ESSAYS

Préférez-vous demeurer en ville ou à la campagne?
Les avantages et les inconvénients de la vie rurale.

See also 11. FARM; 37. TOWN.

8. CRIME—LE CRIME

Crimes

poisoning	**l'empoisonnement (*m.*)**	attempt (on life)	**un attentat (à la vie)**
arson	**le crime d'incendie**	damage	**les dégâts (*m.*)**
larceny	**le larcin**	juvenile delinquency	**la délinquance juvénile**
suicide	**le suicide**	troubles, disturbance	**les troubles (*m.*)**
theft	**le vol**	raid (*by burglars*)	**une attaque**
burglary	**le cambriolage**	raid (*by police*)	**la descente, la rafle**
rape	**le rapt, le viol**	blackmail	**le chantage**
murder	**le meurtre; un assassinat (*planned*)**	capital offence	**le crime capital**

Police and Law

police	**la police**	counsel for the defence	**le défenseur**
policeman	**un agent**	counsel for the prosecution	**le ministère public**
trial	**le procès**	witness box	**la barre des témoins**
jury	**le jury (les jurés —jury-men)**	witness for the defence	**le témoin à décharge**
magistrate	**le magistrat**	witness for the prosecution	**le témoin à charge**
judge	**le juge**		
warder	**le gardien**		
detective	**le détective**		
cross-examination	**un interrogatoire contradictoire**		
third degree	**le passage à tabac**		

Criminals

gangster	**le gangster**	pilferer	**le chipeur**
burglar	**le cambrioleur**	thug	**un apache le bandit**
murderer	**le meurtrier; un assassin**	accused	**un inculpé**
pickpocket	**le voleur à la tire, le pickpocket, le filou**	victim	**la victime**
		sadist	**le sadique**
		accomplice	**le complice**

Punishment

punishment	**la punition, le châtiment**	hard labour	**les travaux forcés**
detention	**la détention**	hanging	**la pendaison**
sentence	**la sentence, la condamnation**	cell	**la cellule**
life imprisonment	**l'emprisonnement (*m.*) à perpétuité**		

Treatment

psychologist	**le psychologue**	rehabilitation centre	**le centre de rééducation**
psycho-analyst	**le psychanalyste**	youth club	**le club de jeunesse**
preventive detention	**la détention préventive**		

Causes

drink	**l'alcoolisme (*m.*)**	housing shortage	**le manque de logements, la crise du logement**
insecurity	**l'insécurité (*f.*)**		
working mothers	**les mères qui travaillent**		
divorce	**le divorce**	broken home	**le foyer désuni**
unsuitable reading	**la mauvaise lecture**	inferiority complex	**la complexe d'infériorité**

The Young Delinquent

delinquent	**le délinquant**	hooligan	**le voyou**
teddy boy	**le blouson noir**	rider of motor-bike	**le motocycliste**
teenager	**un(e) adolescent(e)**	rider of scooter	**le scootériste**
		girl friend	**une petite amie**

Weapons

cosh	**la matraque**	tommy-gun	**la mitraillette**
dagger	**le poignard**	revolver	**le revolver**
flick-knife	**le couteau à cran d'arrêt**		

Adjectives

tough	**dur**	corporal	**corporel**
maladjusted	**mal adapté**	unloved	**mal aimé**
sophisticated	**sophistiqué**		

Verbs

to condemn	condamner
to break in(to houses)	entrer par effraction
to murder	assassiner
to wound	blesser
to stab	poignarder, percer
to set fire to	mettre le feu à
to burgle	cambrioler
to fire upon	tirer sur
to riddle (with bullets)	cribler (de balles)
to execute	exécuter
to hang	pendre
to set free, discharge	libérer, acquitter
to regenerate, reform	régénérer, réformer
to fine	condamner à une amende, frapper d'une amende
to knock down, stun	assommer

Phrases

to take a statement	prendre une déposition
to have a chip on one's shoulder	chercher noise (à quelqu' un), en avoir contre (quelqu'un, la vie)
to carry weapons	porter des armes
to make a raid on a bank	attaquer une banque
to belabour with bicycle chains	assommer à coups de chaîne de bicyclette
the shot went off	le coup partit
there was a crackle of fire	des coups de feu crépitèrent
the police put the handcuffs on him	la police lui passa les menottes
this brings the number of murders in London up to seven	cela porte à sept le nombre des meurtres commis à Londres
to raise the school-leaving age	prolonger la scolarité
both parents go out to work	les parents travaillent tous les deux
to give a wolf whistle	donner un coup de sifflet approbateur, d'admiration
sentenced to two months' imprisonment	condamné à deux mois de prison
the appeal for mercy was turned down	le recours en grâce fut rejeté
to grant a stay of execution	accorder un sursis d'exécution
he was reprieved at the eleventh hour	la peine capitale fut commuée à la onzième heure
to be an advocate of capital punishment	être partisan de la peine capitale
to abolish the death sentence	supprimer la peine de mort
prevention is better than cure	mieux vaut prévenir que guérir
to answer for one's crimes	répondre de ses crimes

ESSAYS

Un vol.
La peine de mort.
La délinquance juvénile—les causes et le remède.

9. CYCLING AND CYCLE RACING—LE CYCLISME

Machine

bicycle	**la bicyclette, le vélo**	bell	**le timbre**
motor-cycle	**la motocyclette**	tyre	**le pneu**
handlebar	**le guidon**	frame	**le cadre**
spoke	**le rayon**	pedal	**la pédale**
brake	**le frein**	carrier	**le porte-bagages**
saddle	**la selle**	pump	**la pompe**
lamp	**le phare**	saddle-bag	**la sacoche**

People

racing cyclist	**le coureur (cycliste)**	sprinter	**le sprinter**
starter	**le starter**	supporter	**le supporter**
follower-up	**le suiveur**	bunch (*of cyclists*)	**le peloton**
		radio commentator	**le radio-reporter**

Racing

race	**la course**	average speed	**la vitesse moyenne**
race-track	**le vélodrome** (*building*); **la piste** (*cycle-track*)	climb	**la montée, la côte**
lap	**le circuit; le tour de piste; une étape** (*road race*)	descent	**la descente**
rest day	**le jour de repos**	acceleration	**la reprise**
		sprint	**le sprint**
		straight	**la ligne droite**

Disaster

puncture	**la crevaison**	fall	**la chute**
skid	**le dérapage**		

Tools, Gear

oil-can	**la burette**	haversack	**la musette (de ravitaillement)**
spanner	**la clef anglaise**	water-bottle	**le bidon**
jersey	**le maillot**	shoes	**les souliers** (*m.*)
shorts	**la culotte, le short**		

Adjectives

mud-spattered	**éclaboussé de boue**	sweaty	**couvert de sueur**
gruelling (*race*)	**éreintant**	all-in	**éreinté**

Verbs

to pass	**dépasser, doubler**	to edge into (*traffic*)	**se faufiler dans**
to catch up	**rattraper**	to sponsor	**patronner**

Phrases

to go cycling	**faire du vélo**
to do 200 kilometres a day	**couvrir 200 kilomètres par jour**
to put up a fine performance	**réaliser une belle performance**
this sport has become very popular	**ce sport a pris un grand essor**
he was all in	**il n'en pouvait plus**
the two machines collided	**les deux machines sont entrées en collision (se sont heurtées)**
to go to the front	**passer en tête**
to sweat profusely	**suer à grosses gouttes**
to win £1000 in prize money	**gagner, remporter, un prix de mille livres sterling**

ESSAYS

Le cyclisme.
Le Tour de France.

See also 21. MOTORING.

10. EDUCATION—L'ÉDUCATION

Lessons and Work

subject	**la matière**	course	**le programme, le cours**
teaching	**l'enseignement (*m.*)**	Arts	**les Humanités (*f.*), les Lettres (*f.*)**
physical education	**l'éducation physique**		
P.T.	**la gymnastique**	Science	**les Sciences (*f.*)**
handwork	**le travail manuel**	Economics	**l'Économie (*f.*) politique**
timetable	**l'emploi (*m.*) du temps**		

Report, Punishment, Crimes

report	**le bulletin (trimestriel); la note (*comment*)**	clout, slap in the face	**la gifle**
		ragging	**le chahut**
imposition	**le pensum**	blame	**le blâme**
detention	**la retenue**	praise	**l'éloge (*m.*), les félicitations (*f.*)**
corporal punishment	**la punition corporelle**		

Functions, Dates

return to school	**la rentrée des classes**	half term	**le congé de mi-trimestre**
prize day, speech day	**la distribution des prix**	long vacation	**les grandes vacances**

People

teachers (*in general*)	**les enseignants, le personnel enseignant**	part-time teacher	**le professeur à mi-temps**
headmaster	**le proviseur** (*in lycée*); **le directeur** (*in other schools*); **le principal** (*in 'collèges'*)	examiner	**un examinateur**
headmistress	**la directrice**	Minister of Education	**le Ministre de l'Éducation Nationale**
schoolmaster, schoolmistress	**le professeur** (*m. and f.*) (*secondary*)	supervisor	**le surveillant**
teacher	**un instituteur, une institutrice** (*primary*)	boarder	**un(e) interne, un(e) pensionnaire**
second master	**le censeur** (*lycée*)	day boy, day girl	**un(e) externe**
		weekly boarder	**un(e) demi-pensionnaire**
		infant prodigy	**un(e) enfant prodige**
		prizewinner	**le lauréat**

Types of School and Classes

nursery school	**une école maternelle**	boarding school	**le pensionnat, un internat, la pension**
primary school	**une école primaire**	day school	**un externat**
secondary school	**le lycée** (*grammar*); **le collège** (*municipal*)	first form	**la sixième**
private school	**une école libre; un collège libre**	lower sixth form	**la première**
		upper sixth form	**la terminale**

College and University

training college	**une école normale**	tutor	**le répétiteur**
professor	**le professeur d'université**	lecture	**la conférence**
lecturer	**le maître de conférences**	student life	**la vie estudiantine**

Examinations

examination	**un examen**	school-leaving certificate	**le baccalauréat**
oral test	**une épreuve orale**	entrance examination	**un examen d'entrée**
scholarship examination	**le concours des bourses**	doctor's thesis	**la thèse de doctorat**
degree	**les grades** (*m.*): **la licence** (*bachelor's degree*)	intelligence test	**le test mental, d'intelligence**

Rooms and Furniture

refectory	**le réfectoire**	prep. room, schoolroom	**la salle d'étude**, **la salle de classe**
dormitory	**le dortoir**	dais	**une estrade**
main hall	**la grande salle**	teacher's desk	**la chaire**
playground	**la cour de récréation**		

Equipment, Clothes

notice-board (*baize*)	le tableau d'affichage, d'annonces
duster	le chiffon, le torchon
blotting-paper	le papier buvard
ball-point pen	le stylo à bille
satchel	le cartable
note-book	le carnet
drawing-board	la planche à dessin
waste-paper basket	la corbeille à papier
pupil's file, record	le dossier d'élève
shorts	la culotte, le short
blazer	le blazer
overall	la blouse, le tablier
gown	la robe, la toge

Adjectives

well-behaved	sage
mischievous	espiègle
hard-working	assidu, travailleur
strict	sévère
well-up, well-versed (in)	ferré (sur), calé (en, sur)
naughty	méchant, polisson
overloaded	surchargé
of the school (*e.g., life, discipline*)	scolaire
of the university	universitaire

Verbs

to swot, swot for (*exam.*)	bûcher
to rag	chahuter
to progress	progresser, faire des progrès
to overwork (*trans.*)	surmener
to sit for (*exam.*)	passer, subir
to pass (an exam.)	réussir, être reçu (à un examen)
to fail (*intrans.*)	échouer, être refusé, être collé
to plough (*candidates*)	recaler
to sit again	être repêché
to learn	apprendre
to teach	enseigner, apprendre (qqc. à qqn.)
to select (*candidate*)	sélectionner
to train	former, dresser
to put down (*one's son for a public school*)	inscrire

Phrases

to play truant	faire l'école buissonnière
to do one's teacher-training	faire son stage, étudier dans une Ecole Normale
to work hard	travailler dur
to be thoroughly bored	s'ennuyer ferme
to be among the prizewinners	être inscrit au palmarès
to raise the school-leaving age	prolonger la scolarité
out-of-school activities	les activités extra-scolaires
he's hopeless at French	il est nul en français
to be sent out of the room	être mis à la porte

ESSAYS

Les années d'école: l'âge le plus heureux de la vie.
Quelques différences entre l'enseignement en France et en Angleterre.
Les examens—sont-ils nécessaires?
Votre école idéale.
La co-éducation.
Notre enseignement est-il trop spécialisé?

Les dangers d'une éducation consacrée à la technologie.
Les qualités du professeur idéal.
Que pensez-vous de l'éducation que vous avez reçue?
Comment tire-t-on le meilleur profit des années de 'Sixth-Form'?
A votre avis, quel devrait être l'âge limite de la scolarité?
L'influence des examens sur notre éducation.
Êtes-vous pour ou contre l'uniforme scolaire?
L'existence des 'Public-Schools' se justifie-t-elle?
'Dans l'éducation moderne on lit trop de livres et on ne pense pas assez.' Discutez.
Pourquoi je veux entrer à une université.
Le rôle de la télévision dans l'enseignement.

11. THE FARM—LA FERME

Work

ploughing	**le labour, le labourage**	harvesting, harvest	**la moisson (*cereals*), la récolte (*fruit*)**
sowing	**les semailles (*f.*), l'ensemencement (*m.*)**	cultivation	**la culture (*in pl.* = land under cultivation)**
haymaking	**la fenaison**		
rearing	**l'élevage (*m.*)**	feeding	**l'alimentation (*f.*) (du bétail)**

People

farmer	**le fermier; le cultivateur; un agriculteur (*in economic, industrial sense*)**	ploughman	**le laboureur**
		shepherd	**le berger**
		market-gardener	**le maraîcher**
labourer	**l'ouvrier, le valet de ferme**		

Animals

cattle, livestock	**le bétail**	pig; sow	**le cochon, le porc; la truie**
goat	**la chèvre**		
mare	**la jument**	carthorse	**le cheval de trait**
calf	**le veau**	a team of oxen	**un attelage de bœufs**

Produce

foodstuffs	**les aliments (*m.*), les denrées (*f.*) (alimentaires)**	clover	**le trèfle**
		hay	**le foin**
		vine	**la vigne**
grain crops	**les céréales (*,.*)**	oil-seed plants	**les oléagineux (*m.*)**
corn	**le blé**		
wheat	**le froment**	fodder	**le fourrage**
barley	**l'orge (*f.*)**	rick	**la meule (de foin)**
oats	**l'avoine (*f.*)**	stook	**le tas de gerbes, la moyette**
rye	**le seigle**		
maize	**le maïs**	sheaf	**la gerbe**
straw	**la paille**	flour	**la farine**
stubble	**le chaume**		

Parts of Farm

field	**le champ** (*ploughed*); **le pré, la prairie, le pâturage** (*under grass*)	well	**le puits**
barn	**la grange**	dairy	**la laiterie**
shed	**le hangar**	gate	**la barrière**
cowshed, byre	**une étable**	fence	**la palissade, la clôture**
stable	**une écurie**	land, soil	**le sol, la terre**
farmyard	**la basse-cour**	furrow	**le sillon**
kennel	**la niche**	arable land	**la terre labourable, la terre arable**
		pasture	**les pâturages** (*m.*)

Poultry

poultry	**la volaille**	chicken	**le poussin** (*just hatched*), **le poulet**
duck	**le canard, la cane**	turkey	**le dindon, la dinde**
duckling	**le caneton**		
goose	**une oie**		
cock	**le coq**		
hen	**la poule**		

Machinery, Tools

plough	**la charrue**	motor lorry	**le camion**
tractor	**le tracteur**	cart	**la charrette**
combine-harvester	**la moissonneuse-batteuse**	yoke	**le joug**
milking machine	**la machine à traire, la trayeuse**	harrow	**la herse**
		pitchfork	**la fourche**

Seeds and Fertilisers

seed	**la graine, la semence**	fertiliser (*artificial*)	**l'engrais (chimique)**
manure	**l'engrais** (*m.*) (*solid*); **le purin** (*liquid*)	dung	**le fumier**

Disease, Evils

foot and mouth disease	**la fièvre aphteuse**	drought	**la sécheresse**

Economics

guaranteed prices	**les prix garantis**	wages	**le salaire**
subsidy	**la subvention**	profits	**les bénéfices** (*m.*)
yield	**le rendement**	competition	**la concurrence**
production	**la production (agricole)**	co-operative	**la coopérative**

Adjectives

fertile	**fertile**	heavy (*soil*)	**lourd**
dry	**aride**	light (*soil*)	**léger, meuble**
barren	**stérile**		

Verbs

to rear	élever
to till	cultiver
to plough	labourer
to fertilise	fertiliser
to sow	semer
to grow	cultiver (*trans.*), pousser (*intrans.*)
to milk	traire
to shear	tondre
to feed (*animals*)	donner à manger à, alimenter
to water	abreuver
to bring in (*cattle*), to gather (*harvest*)	rentrer
to turn over (*earth*)	retourner
to ripen (*intrans.*)	mûrir
to lay (eggs)	pondre (des œufs)
to produce	produire
to consume	consommer
to thresh	battre

Phrases
(*Life*)

to be soaked to the skin	être trempé jusqu'aux os
to inhale the fresh air	humer l'air frais
to involve heavy labour	impliquer un travail dur
to throw handfuls of maize to the chickens	lancer aux poules le maïs à pleines poignées
to put in countless hours in the fields	faire des heures innombrables dans les champs
to make hay on a sunny morning	faire les foins par un matin ensoleillé

(*Economics*)

to save labour	économiser la main-d'œuvre
to keep up one's standard of living	maintenir son niveau de vie
conditions have improved	les conditions se sont améliorées
the farm used to have a derelict look	la ferme avait un air d'abandon
to have a bumper harvest	avoir une grosse récolte
to fear competition	craindre la concurrence
to put land under grass	mettre le terrain en herbe

(*Description*)

fields stretching endlessly away (as far as the eye can see)	les champs qui s'étendent à l'infini (à perte de vue)
to have superb views	avoir de belles perspectives

(*Weather*)

the days are visibly drawing in	les jours raccourcissent à vue d'œil
heavy black clouds pile up on the horizon	de gros nuages noirs s'amoncellent à l'horizon

ESSAYS

Une journée d'un fermier.
'Le métier de fermier est un des plus agréables du monde.' Discutez.
La ferme moderne.

See also 7. COUNTRYSIDE; 15. GARDEN.

12. FIRE SERVICE—LE SERVICE D'INCENDIE

Station and Equipment

fire station	le caserne de pompiers (d'incendie)	motor ladder	une échelle mobile
fire engine	la pompe à incendie	mobile pump	la pompe baladeuse
fire alarm	une alerte d'incendie, un avertisseur d'incendie	jet of water	le jet d'eau
control room	la salle de contrôle	helmet	le casque
		Wellington boots	les bottes (*f.*) en caoutchouc
		hose	le tuyau
		safety net	la toile de sauvetage

People

fireman	le pompier (le sapeur-pompier)	badly burned person	un(e) brûlé(e)
victim	la victime	rescuer	le sauveteur

Fire

fire	le feu, le sinistre	column of smoke	la colonne de fumée
blaze, conflagration	l'incendie (*m.*), l'embrasement (*m.*)	spark	une étincelle
wreath of smoke	la spirale (la volute) de fumée		

Rescue

safety exit	une issue de secours	rescue operation	le sauvetage

Verbs

to catch fire	prendre feu	to unwind (*hose*)	dérouler
to panic	s'affoler	to risk (*life*)	risquer
to break out (*fires*)	se déclarer	to fly (*sparks*)	jaillir
to plunge into mourning	endeuiller	to be fireproof	être à l'épreuve du feu
to spread (*fire*)	se propager, s'étendre	to evacuate	évacuer
to control (*fire*)	maîtriser		

Phrases

fire!	au feu!
there's a smell of burning	il y a une odeur de brûlé
to have small regard for danger	faire peu de cas du danger
he came down the ladder with the girl over his shoulder	il a descendu l'échelle, la jeune fille sur l'épaule
to behave like a hero	se conduire en héros
no one knows how the fire started	on ignore comment le feu a pris naissance

the neighbourhood became a hell of fire and smoke	**le voisinage a été transformé en un enfer de flammes et de fumée**
the safety exit was blocked	**la sortie de secours était bloquée**
countless heroic acts	**de nombreux actes d'héroïsme**
a badly burned child	**un enfant grièvement brûlé**
crushed by falling timbers	**écrasé par la charpente qui s'effondrait**
panic gripped the children	**la panique s'est emparée des enfants**
to look for a way of escape	**chercher une issue pour s'échapper**
a burning fiery furnace	**une fournaise ardente**
I witnessed heartrending scenes	**j'ai été témoin de scènes déchirantes**
to rummage among the ruins	**fouiller parmi les décombres**
damage estimated at millions of francs	**des dégâts évalués à des millions de francs**
to blaze away	**flamber comme une torche**
to go up in smoke	**s'envoler en fumée**
to be burned alive (to death)	**être brûlé vif**

ESSAY

Un incendie.

13. FOOTBALL—LE FOOTBALL et LE RUGBY

1. *Le Football*

Parts of the Field

pitch	**le terrain**	cross-bar	**la barre**
half-way line	**la ligne médiane**	net	**le filet**
touch-line	**la ligne de touche**	corner flag	**le poteau de coin, de corner**
goal	**le but, le goal**		
post	**le montant, le poteau**		

Players

goalkeeper	**le gardien de but**	linesman	**le juge de touche**
right back	**l'arrière droit**	forward line	**la ligne d'attaque**
left back	**l'arrière gauche**	team mate	**le coéquipier**
right half	**le demi droit**	reserve	**le remplaçant**
centre half	**le demi centre**	footballer	**le footballeur, le joueur de football**
left half	**le demi gauche**		
right wing	**l'ailier droit**		
inside right	**l'inter droit**	trainer, coach	**un entraîneur**
centre forward	**l'avant centre**	spectator	**le spectateur**
inside left	**l'inter gauche**	supporter	**le supporter**
outside left	**l'ailier gauche**	opponent	**un adversaire**
referee	**un arbitre**	the local side	**les locaux (*m.*)**

The Ground

stand	**la tribune**	floodlights	**les projecteurs (*m.*)**
terrace	**les gradins (*m.*)**		
cloakroom	**le vestiaire**	turnstile	**le tourniquet**

The Play

toss-up	le tirage au sort	extra time	la prolongation
match	le match (*pl.* les matchs, les matches)	resumption	la reprise
		free kick	le coup franc
		penalty	le penalty (la pénalité)
meeting, encounter	la rencontre	corner	le corner
kick-off	le coup d'envoi	goal	le but
kick	le coup de pied	score	le score
header	le coup de tête	charge	la charge
play	le jeu	tactics	la tactique
out of play	hors-jeu	ball control	le contrôle du ballon
half-time	la mi-temps		

Equipment

ball	le ballon (*Rugby:* la balle)	shorts	la culotte
		stockings, socks	les bas (*m.*)
boot	la chaussure, le soulier	shin-guard	la jambière
		boot-lace	le lacet
jersey	le maillot	rattle	la crécelle

Adjectives

exciting	passionnant	fit	au point, en bonne forme
well-balanced	équilibré		
opposing	adverse	dirty (game)	pas propre, brutal

Verbs

to head	jouer de la tête	to trip	faire un croc-en-jambe (à)
to pass	passer		
to shoot	shooter	to send sprawling	renverser
to dribble	dribbler, faire un dribbling	to boo	huer

Phrases

a real master of ball control	un vrai virtuose du ballon
to (play a) draw	faire match nul
the two captains tossed: Duflos won	les deux capitaines ont tiré au sort: Duflos a gagné
to be at full strength	être au complet
to lie well back	se tenir en retrait
to show splendid form	faire preuve d'une forme splendide
to throw orange peel at the ref.	jeter des pelures d'orange à l'arbitre
to score an equaliser	marquer un but égalisateur
to fill the outside left position	être au poste d'ailier gauche
what's the line-up?	quelle est la composition de l'équipe?
to have a kick-about	taper dans le ballon
that ref. spoils the play with too much whistle	cet arbitre gâche le jeu par de trop nombreux coups de sifflet
to have a two-goal lead	mener par deux buts

to try one's luck (try a shot)	**tenter sa chance**
to be standing (round the ground)	**être aux pourtours**
to get to the fourth round of the Cup	**arriver jusqu'au quatrième tour de la Coupe**
the takings from this game were excellent	**ce match nous a valu une grosse recette**
to undergo a severe training programme	**subir un entraînement rigoureux**
go it, Higginbotham!	**vas-y, Higginbotham!**
to have a broken leg	**avoir la jambe fracturée, cassée**
to bring back the crowds	**ramener la foule**

2. *Le Rugby*

Players

rugby player	**le rugby-man (*pl.* les rugby-men), le joueur de rugby**	back	**un arrière**
full back	**un arrière**	forward	**un avant, un pilier**
three-quarters	**le trois-quarts**	front row	**la ligne d'attaque, la première ligne**
right wing-three-quarter	**le trois-quarts aile droite**	lock forward	**la rentrée en mêlée**
right centre	**le centre droit**	hooker	**le talonneur**
scrum half	**le demi de mêlée**	touch judge	**le juge de touche**
stand-off half	**le demi d'ouverture**	scorer	**le marqueur**

Parts of the Field

touch-line	**la ligne de touche**	goal line	**la ligne de but**
dead ball line	**la ligne de ballon mort**		

Play

line-out	**la ligne**	foul	**la faute**
run	**la course**	try	**un essai**
breakaway	**une échappée**	goal	**un but (sur essai)**
scrum	**la mêlée**	penalty goal	**un but (sur coup franc)**
knock-on	**le coup de pied à suivre**	drop goal	**le drop**
forward pass	**la passe en avant**		

Verbs

to tackle	**plaquer**	to outrun	**prendre quelqu'un de vitesse**
to score a try	**marquer (un essai)**	to cross (the line)	**franchir (les buts)**
to convert	**transformer (un essai)**	to pierce (the defence)	**trouer (la défense)**
to drop (a goal)	**réussir un drop**	to heel out	**talonner**
to back up, support	**redoubler**	to penalise	**sanctionner**
to dodge (*intrans.*)	**crocheter**	to break away	**se dégager**
to pass (*ball*)	**passer**	to kick to touch	**botter en touche**
to feint	**feinter**	to knock on	**pousser la balle en avant**

Phrases

to take the ball on the bounce	**prendre la balle au rebond**
the acrid smell in the scrum	**l'âcre odeur de la mêlée**
we had 23 points to our credit	**nous avions vingt-trois points à notre actif**
mud-spattered players	**des joueurs éclaboussés de boue**
he's the world's best place-kicker	**c'est le plus formidable coup de pied du monde**
what rotten reffing!	**quel mauvais arbitrage!**

ESSAYS

Football ou Rugby?
Un match passionnant auquel j'ai participé (*ou*, que j'ai vu).
Le Football international—favorise-t-il l'amitié entre les nations?

14. FOREIGN TRADE—LE COMMERCE EXTÉRIEUR

Essentials

imports	**les importations (*f.*)**	tariff barriers	**les barrières douanières**
exports	**les exportations (*f.*)**	outlets	**les débouchés (*m.*)**
		markets	**les marchés (*m.*)**
tariffs	**les droits (*m.*) de douane**	quota	**le contingent; le quota**

Principles

competition	**la concurrence**	preferential tariff	**le tarif, le droit différentiel, préférentiel**
discrimination	**la discrimination**		

Trade Groups

the Six (Common Market, European Community)	**les Six (le Marché Commun, la Communauté Européenne): la France, la Belgique, la Hollande, le Luxembourg, l'Allemagne, l'Italie**	the Seven	**les Sept: la Grande-Bretagne, la Suède, la Norvège, le Danemark, la Suisse, le Portugal l'Autriche**
		block	**le bloc**
		unit	**une unité**

Trade Group Objectives

covenant	**une convention**	freedom of movement (for workers)	**la libre circulation (des travailleurs)**
agreement	**un accord**	(for capital)	**(des capitaux)**
treaty	**un traité**	High Authority (for coal)	**la Haute Autorité (du Charbon)**
objective	**un objectif**	supra-nationality	**la supranationalité**
customs union	**une union douanière**		
free trade zone	**la zone de libre-échange**		
lower prices	**les prix réduits**		

Possible Objectives

common currency	**la monnaie commune**	Channel Tunnel	**Le Tunnel sous La Manche**
influential position (with regard to)	**une situation privilégiée (vis-à-vis de)**	a Third Force	**une Troisième Force**

Goods

atomic energy	**l'énergie(*f.*) atomique**	manufactured goods	**les produits manufacturés**
coal	**le charbon**	farm products	**les produits agricoles**
steel	**l'acier (*m.*)**		
iron ore	**le minerai de fer**	raw materials	**les matières premières**

People

consumer	**le consommateur**	business man	**un homme d'affaires**
producer	**le producteur**		
farmer	**un agriculteur**	trade unionist	**le syndicaliste**
industrialist	**un industriel**	horticulturist	**un horticulteur**
worker	**le travailleur**		

Adjectives

hostile	**hostile**	isolated, out of it	**isolé**
stubborn	**intransigeant**		

Verbs

to absorb (*exports*)	**absorber**	to give up (sovereignty)	**abandonner (la souveraineté)**
to negotiate	**négocier**	to stimulate	**stimuler**
to be against	**s'opposer à**	to cure	**remédier à**
to increase (exports)	**accroître (les exportations)**	to balance (*imports and exports*)	**équilibrer**

Phrases

the signatories of the treaty	**les signataires du traité**
to be a non-member country	**être un pays non-membre**
links with the Commonwealth	**les liens avec le Commonwealth**
British Trade Unions fear foreign workers coming in	**les syndicats britanniques redoutent l'entrée des travailleurs étrangers**
we shall be inundated with cheap farm produce	**nous serons inondés de produits agricoles à bas prix**
goods coming from the Continent	**les marchandises en provenance du Continent**
our insularity has something to do with it	**notre insularité y est pour quelque chose**
a decline in British economic prosperity	**un déclin dans la prospérité économique de la Grande-Bretagne**
short (long) term interest	**les intérêts à courte (longue) échéance**
improved living standards	**un niveau de vie amélioré**
a new era of prosperity	**une nouvelle ère de prospérité**

overseas investments	les placements outre-mer
gradual reduction of tariffs	une réduction graduelle des droits de douane
to have favourable repercussions (on)	avoir des répercussions favorables (sur)
to come into force	entrer en vigueur
to be a bridge (between two groups)	constituer un pont (entre deux groupes)
to help under-developed countries	porter aide aux pays sous-développés
to weaken the influence of Communism	affaiblir l'influence du Communisme
to take protective measures	prendre des mesures de protection

ESSAYS

La Grande-Bretagne et le Marché Commun.
Que devrions-nous faire pour accroître nos exportations?
'Britain must export or die.' Est-ce vrai?

15. THE GARDEN—LE JARDIN

Types

kitchen garden	le jardin potager	rock garden	le jardin de rocaille
orchard	le verger	cold frame	le châssis de couches
greenhouse	la serre		

Tools

trowel	la houlette, le transplantoir	fork	la fourche
		rake	le râteau
hoe	la houe, la binette	barrow	la brouette
lawn-mower	la tondeuse (à gazon)	watering-can	un arrosoir
		hose	le tuyau
roller	le rouleau	incinerator	un incinérateur
spade	la bêche		

Accessories to Garden

hammock	le hamac	pond	le bassin
summer-house	le pavillon	seat	le banc

Parts of Garden

fence	la clôture	lawn	la pelouse
path	une allée	hedge	la haie
flower bed	le parterre; la plate-bande	crazy paving	le dallage irrégulier

Trees

fruit tree	un arbre fruitier	beech	le hêtre
birch	le bouleau	copper beech	le hêtre rouge
box	le buis	yew	un if
chestnut	le marronnier; le châtaignier (*edible chestnut*)	lilac	le lilas
		elm	un orme
		poplar	le peuplier
oak	le chêne	sycamore	le sycomore
maple	un érable	fir	le sapin
ash	le frêne	holly	le houx

Bushes, Shrubs

bush	**le buisson**	ivy	le lierre
shrub	**un arbuste**		

Flowers

dandelion	**le pissenlit**	hyacinth	la jacinthe
pansy	**la pensée**	daisy	la marguerite; la pâquerette (*common*)
rose-bush	**le rosier**	tulip	la tulipe
poppy	**le coquelicot** (*wild*); **le pavot** (*cultivated*)	daffodil	la jonquille, le narcisse sauvage des bois
carnation	**un œillet**	bunch	le bouquet
wallflower	**la giroflée jaune**		

Fruit

cherry	**la cerise**	apple	la pomme
plum	**la prune**	pear	la poire

Soft Fruit

raspberry	**la framboise**	redcurrant	la groseille rouge
strawberry	**la fraise**	gooseberry	la groseille à maquereau
blackcurrant	**le cassis**		

Parts of Plant and Tree

root	**la racine**	branch	la branche
stem, stalk	**la tige**	bough	le rameau
leaf	**la feuille**	berry	la baie
bud	**le bourgeon**	blade (of grass)	le brin (d'herbe)
trunk	**le tronc**		

Weeds

weed	**la mauvaise herbe**	bonfire	le feu de joie, le feu d'herbes
nettle	**une ortie**		

Soils

clay	**l'argile (*f.*)**	sand	le sable
chalk	**la craie**	soil	le sol

Vegetables and Herbs

cabbage	**le chou**	spinach	l'épinard (*m.*)
cauliflower	**le chou-fleur** (*pl.* **choux-fleurs**)	artichoke	un artichaut
bean	**le haricot; le haricot vert** (*green runner-bean*)	celery	le céleri
		beetroot	la betterave
		tomato	la tomate
		onion	un oignon
peas	**les petits pois**	cucumber	le concombre
carrot	**la carotte**	lettuce	la laitue
turnip	**le navet**	mint	la menthe
radish	**le radis**	parsley	le persil

Adjectives

fragrant	odorant	back-breaking	éreintant

Verbs

to grow (*trans.*)	cultiver	to keep up	maintenir, entretenir
to grow (*intrans.*)	pousser		
to open out	s'épanouir	to prune	émonder (*tree*); tailler (*bush*)
to fade	se faner		
to wither	se flétrir	to dig	creuser, piocher
to mow	tondre; faucher	to sting, prick	piquer
to water	arroser	to neglect	négliger
to pick	cueillir	to weed	désherber
to sow (seeds)	semer (les graines)	to sweep up	balayer

Phrases

a marvellous crop of weeds	une superbe récolte de mauvaises herbes
to be all of a sweat	être tout en nage
to break your back	s'éreinter
to sigh for a cold drink	réclamer un verre d'eau fraîche
to bend double	se courber en deux
to get blood pressure	avoir de la tension
to throw bricks over the wall	jeter des briques par-dessus le mur
to escape from the outside world	s'échapper du monde extérieur
to watch the flowers grow	regarder pousser les fleurs
to take tea on the lawn	goûter sur la pelouse
in the shade of the old apple tree	à l'ombre du vieux pommier
that bed was a blaze of colour last week	la semaine dernière ce parterre était une orgie de couleurs
with lashings of fertiliser	à grand renfort d'engrais
to have a wonderful show of dahlias	avoir un déploiement magnifique de dahlias

ESSAYS

Les plaisirs du jardinage.
Mon jardin.

16. HOLIDAYS AND TRAVEL—LES VACANCES (*f.*) ET LES VOYAGES (*m.*)

Types of Holiday

family holidays	les vacances en famille	paid holidays	le congé payé
exchange visit	une visite d'échange	a pleasure trip	un voyage d'agrément
a day's relaxation	un jour de repos, de détente	cruise	une croisière
an afternoon off	un(e) après-midi de libre	health cure	la cure
		the off season	la morte-saison

People

holiday-maker — **le vacancier**
tourist — **le (la) touriste**
exchange scholar — **un(e) élève d'échange**
paying guest — **un hôte payant**
summer visitor — **un(e) estivant(e)**
winter visitor — **un(e) hivernant(e)**
camper — **le campeur**
youth hosteller — **un(e) ajiste**
customs officer — **le douanier**
hotel manager — **le gérant**
chambermaid — **la femme de chambre**
page-boy, bell-hop — **le chasseur, le groom**
lift attendant — **le liftier (la liftière)**

Preparations

preparation — **le préparatif**
travel agency — **le bureau de tourisme (une agence de voyage)**
label (sticky) — **une étiquette (gommée)**
route — **un itinéraire**
passport — **le passeport**
trunk — **la malle**
bag — **la valise, le sac**
timetable (*book*) — **un indicateur**

Outdoor Holiday

camping — **le camping**
caravan — **la caravane** (*towed*); **la roulotte** (*motorised*)
youth hostel — **une auberge de jeunesse**
hiking — **le marche à pied le footing**
rucksack — **le sac à dos**
portable stove — **le réchaud portatif**
ground-sheet — **le tapis de sol**
sleeping-bag — **le sac de couchage**

Money

tip — **le pourboire**
traveller's cheque — **le chèque de voyage**
fare — **le prix du voyage**
exchange rate — **le taux du change**
note — **le billet**
change — **la (petite) monnaie**

Adjectives

cultural — **culturel**
home-loving — **casanier**
far-off — **éloigné**
costly — **coûteux**
modestly priced — **à prix modéré**

Verbs

to book — **réserver, retenir**
to hike — **faire du footing, du tourisme à pied**
to hitch-hike — **faire de l'auto-stop**
to gape, goggle at — **regarder bouche bée**
to pack — **emballer**
to unpack — **déballer**
to label — **étiqueter**
to find one's way about — **s'orienter**
to note, observe — **constater**
to find out (about) — **se renseigner (sur)**

Phrases

to be broad-minded — **avoir les idées larges**
to have attractions for — **avoir des attraits, des charmes, pour**
to make a fool of oneself — **se rendre ridicule**
to improve one's knowledge — **perfectionner sa connaissance**

to broaden one's outlook	**élargir ses connaissances (son horizon)**
to increase international understanding	**faciliter les bons rapports internationaux**
to have educative value	**avoir une valeur éducative**
to have the wanderlust	**avoir la manie des voyages, avoir la bougeotte**
a rolling stone gathers no moss	**pierre qui roule n'amasse pas mousse**
to fight against prejudice	**combattre les préjugés**
to learn at first hand the foreign way of life	**apprendre à connaître par soi-même les mœurs étrangères**
to be at the mercy of some dishonest taxi-driver	**être à la merci d'un chauffeur de taxi malhonnête**
I can't afford to go by air	**je n'ai pas les moyens de voyager par avion**
a cheap form of travel	**un moyen économique de voyager**
to have Saturday off	**faire la semaine anglaise**
to travel at low cost	**voyager à peu de frais**
to go touring in the U.S.A.	**voyager dans les U.S.A.**
to be on holiday (*sea*, *country*)	**être en villégiature**
to reduce one's luggage to a minimum	**réduire ses bagages au minimum**

ESSAYS

La valeur des voyages à l'étranger.
L'Anglais à l'étranger.
Les vacances les plus agréables que j'aie passées.
Les vacances en l'an 2060.
Le camping.
S'il vous était possible d'aller passer un mois en France, où iriez-vous? Donnez vos raisons.
Quel intérêt l'Angleterre offre-t-elle au touriste étranger?
Les avantages et les désavantages des vacances en famille.
L'étalement des vacances (staggered holidays).
S'il vous fallait émigrer, où iriez-vous, et pourquoi?
Comment créer des liens plus étroits entre l'Angleterre et la France?

See also 33. SEASIDE.

17. HOUSE—LA MAISON

Rooms

dining-room	**la salle à manger**	scullery	**l'arrière-cuisine** (*f.*)
lounge	**le salon**	larder	**le garde-manger**
hall	**le vestibule**	pantry	**le garde-manger, une office**
study	**le cabinet de travail, le bureau**	spare room	**la chambre d'amis**
kitchen	**la cuisine**	cellar	**la cave**
W.C.	**les cabinets, les waters** (*m.*), **les toilettes** (*f.*)	library	**la bibliothèque**
playroom	**la chambre d'enfants**	bedroom	**la chambre à coucher**
attic	**la mansarde**	sun lounge	**la véranda**
loft	**le grenier**	back room	**la chambre sur le derrière**

Exterior

front	**la façade**	drain-pipe	**le tuyau de descente**
back	**le derrière**	front door	**la porte d'entrée**
gable	**le pignon**	front gate	**le portail**
eaves	**l'avant-toit (*m.*)**		
gutter	**la gouttière**		

Furniture

arm-chair	**le fauteuil**	dressing table	**la table de toilette**
settee	**le divan**	bedside rug	**la descente de lit**
writing-desk	**le bureau (le secrétaire)**	single bed	**le lit pour une personne**
drawer	**le tiroir**	double bed	**le lit pour deux personnes, un grand lit**
sideboard	**le buffet**	chest of drawers	**la commode**
cupboard	**une armoire**	bed-settee, put-you-up	**le canapé-lit**
wall cupboard	**le placard**		
wardrobe	**une armoire à glace**		

Other Parts of House

lift	**un ascenseur**	landing	**le palier**
balcony	**le balcon**	partition	**la cloison**
tile	**le carreau, la tuile**	ceiling	**le plafond**
pane	**le carreau, la vitre**	floor	**le plancher, le parquet (*wooden*)**
mantelpiece	**le dessus de la cheminée, le manteau de la cheminée**	ground floor	**le rez-de-chaussée**
staircase	**un escalier**	basement	**le sous-sol**
doorsteps	**le perron**	first floor	**le premier étage**
step	**la marche**	front door	**la porte d'entrée**
balustrade	**la rampe**	back door	**la porte de service**

Fitments

door knob	**la poignée (de porte)**	shelf, bookcase	**une étagère**
hinge	**le gond**	door knocker	**le marteau (de porte)**
lock	**la serrure**	electric bell	**la sonnette électrique**
bolt	**le verrou**	service hatch	**le passe-plats**
blind	**le store**	window-box	**la caisse à fleurs, la jardinière**
shutter	**le volet**	cushion	**le coussin**
bedside lamp	**la lampe de chevet**	upholstery	**la tapisserie**
lamp-shade	**un abat-jour**	tablecloth	**la nappe**
standard lamp	**le lampadaire**	table-cover	**le tapis (de table)**
tap	**le robinet**	cooker	**la cuisinière**
towel rail	**le porte-serviettes; le séchoir (*heated*)**	oven	**le four**
bath	**la baignoire**	point	**la prise**
wash-basin	**la cuvette**	gas stove	**le fourneau à gaz**
wash-stand	**le lavabo**	gewgaw, knick-knack	**le bibelot**

Labour-saving Devices

boiler	**la chaudière**
washing-up machine	**la machine à laver la vaisselle**
floor polisher	**la cireuse**
sewing machine	**la machine à coudre**
vacuum cleaner	**un aspirateur**
washing machine	**la machine à laver**
spin-dryer	**une essoreuse**
refrigerator (fridge)	**le réfrigérateur, le frigidaire (le frigo)**
electric iron	**le fer (à repasser) électrique**
mixer	**le mixer**
mincer	**le hachoir**
stainless steel sink	**un évier en acier inoxydable**
pressure cooker	**l'auto-cuiseur (*m.*)**
coffee percolator	**la cafetière automatique, le percolateur**
coffee grinder	**un moulin à café**
water heater	**le chauffe-eau**
eye-level grill	**le gril**
toaster	**le grille-pain**
electric fire	**le radiateur électrique**
central heating	**le chauffage central au mazout (*oil-fired*); au gaz (*gas-heated*)**
immersion heater	**un chauffe-liquide**
paraffin stove	**le poêle à pétrole**
thermostatic control	**le thermostat**

Luxuries

spring mattress	**le sommier**
fluorescent lighting	**l'éclairage fluorescent**
concealed lighting	**l'éclairage indirect**
water-softener	**un adoucisseur d'eau**
fitted carpet	**un tapis cloué**
electric blanket	**la couverture chauffante**
shower bath	**la douche**
foam-rubber cushions	**les coussins (*m. pl.*) en caoutchouc mousse**
plastic floor covering	**le revêtement (de sol) plastique**
folding partition	**la cloison mobile**
sliding door	**la porte à glissière**

People

householder	**le chef de famille**
landlord	**le propriétaire**
tenant	**le locataire**
builder	**le constructeur**
decorator	**le décorateur**
housewife	**la ménagère**

Types of Residence

villa	**la villa**
flat	**un appartement**
cottage	**la maisonnette; la chaumière (*thatched*)**
caravan	**la caravane; la roulotte (*on wheels*)**
plot	**le terrain**
bungalow	**le bungalow**
subsidised dwelling	**une habitation à loyer modéré**
housing shortage	**la crise du logement**
semi-detached house	**la maison jumelle**

Materials

brick	**la brique**	wall-paper	**le papier peint**
stucco	**le stuc**	plastics	**les matières plastiques** (*f.*)
concrete	**le béton**	chromium	**le chrome**
cement	**le ciment**		
paint	**la peinture**		

Disadvantages

draught	**le courant d'air**	dust	**la poussière**
dirt	**la saleté**	damp	**l'humidité** (*f.*)

Adjectives

uncomfortable	**peu confortable**	in good taste	**de bon goût**
ill-lit	**mal éclairé**	sound-proof	**insonore**
airy	**bien aéré**	home-loving	**casanier**
spacious	**spacieux**	ultra-modern	**ultra-moderne**
well-kept	**bien tenu**	damp-proof	**protégé de l'humidité; hydrofuge** (*wall*)
well-planned	**bien aménagé**		
sunny	**ensoleillé**		
air-conditioned	**climatisé**		

Verbs

to relax	**se détendre**	to open on to	**(s')ouvrir sur**
to save (economise in)	**économiser**	to look on to	**avoir vue sur**
to save (spare)	**épargner**	to lead to	**accéder à**
to dust	**épousseter; dépoussiérer** (*with sweeper*)	to keep house	**tenir la maison, le ménage**
to let in (*light*, *etc.*)	**laisser entrer**	to wash up	**laver (faire) la vaisselle**
to move house	**déménager**	to wash clothes	**faire la lessive**
to move in	**emménager**	to set the table	**mettre le couvert**
to give on to	**donner sur**	to deaden (noise)	**amortir (les bruits)**

Phrases

he lives in the rue Faidherbe	**il habite rue Faidherbe**
to live as one likes	**vivre à sa guise**
an Englishman's home is his castle	**charbonnier est maître chez lui**
to have a house of one's own	**avoir pignon sur rue, être propriétaire**
a lounge on a level with the garden	**un salon de plain-pied avec le jardin**
furniture on rollers	**les meubles à roulettes**
to have a house-warming	**pendre la crémaillère**
to get rid of back-breaking tasks	**se débarrasser des corvées éreintantes**
for too long we have been putting up with . . .	**depuis trop longtemps nous supportons . . .**
detergents that make your linen really white	**les détergents qui rendent le linge vraiment éblouissant**

ESSAYS

Votre maison idéale.
Description de votre maison.
Maison ou appartement; lequel préférez-vous?
Le manque de confort dans la maison anglaise.
'A woman's place is in the home.'
L'importance des économiseurs de travail (labour-saving devices).

18. INDUSTRY—L'INDUSTRIE (*f.*)

Personnel

manufacturer	**le fabricant, un industriel**	factory manager	**le directeur d'usine**
tycoon, magnate, big business man	**le gros industriel, le magnat**	shop steward	**le délégué syndical**
employer	**un employeur; le patron** (*more familiar*)	foreman	**le contremaître**
		worker	**un ouvrier, le travailleur**
		apprentice	**un apprenti**

Groups

the 'bosses', employers	**le patronat**	trade union	**le syndicat**
craftsmen	**l'artisanat** (*m.*)	labour	**la main-d'œuvre**
the 'workers'	**la classe ouvrière** (*social and political*)		

Factory

factory	**la fabrique; une usine; la manufacture** (*large factory*)	workshop	**un atelier**
		workyard, work-site	**le chantier**

Manufactured Goods

synthetic fibres	**les fibres** (*f.*) **synthétiques**	textiles	**les textiles** (*m.*)
plastics	**les plastiques** (*m.*)	manufactured article	**le produit manufacturé**

Power, Fuel, Raw Materials

deposit	**le gisement**	driving power	**la force motrice**
coal (*industrial*)	**la houille**	liquid fuels	**les combustibles** (*m.*) **liquides**
coal (*domestic*)	**le charbon**		
steam	**la vapeur**	iron ore	**le minerai de fer**
hydro-electric power	**la houille blanche**	raw materials	**les matières premières**
atomic power	**l'énergie** (*f.*) **atomique**		

Machinery, Parts of Factory

furnace	**le fourneau**	cafeteria	**la cafeteria**
boiler	**la chaudière**	canteen	**la cantine**
hand lever	**la manette**	stand	**le stand**
conveyor belt	**la courroie transporteuse, le tapis roulant**		

Types of Factory and Industrial Areas

refinery	**la raffinerie**	iron works	**les forges (*f.*)**
steelworks	**une aciérie**	iron smelting (*process and industry*)	**la sidérurgie**
blast furnace	**le haut fourneau**		
loom	**le métier à tisser**		
foundry	**la fonderie**	power station	**la centrale**
coal-mine	**une mine de houille**	key industry	**une industrie-clé**
		industrial area	**la région manufacturière**
spinning-mill	**la filature**		
weaving-mill	**le tissage**	mining area	**la région minière**
brewery	**la brasserie**		

Working Conditions

part-time work	**le travail à mi-temps**	public holiday	**le jour férié**
		paid holidays	**les congés payés**
overtime	**les heures supplémentaires**	piece-work	**le travail aux pièces**
working day	**le jour ouvrable**	slack season	**la morte-saison**
regular employment	**la stabilité d'emploi**	break	**la pause**

Industrial Ups and Downs

boom	**le boom**	recession	**le ralentissement la récession**
slump	**la crise**		
		recovery	**la reprise**

Economics

investment	**le placement**	loss	**la perte**
wages	**le salaire**	output	**la production, le rendement**
salary	**le traitement**		
profit	**le bénéfice**		

Labour and Labour Troubles

lock-out	**le lock-out**	industrial unrest	**une agitation ouvrière**
strike	**la grève**		
striker	**le gréviste**	manpower shortage	**la pénurie de main-d'œuvre**
unemployment	**le chômage**		
unemployed man	**le chômeur**	manpower surplus	**la pléthore, le surplus, de main-d'œuvre**
unemployment benefit	**les allocations (*f.*) de chômage**		
family allowances	**les allocations familiales**	labour market	**le marché du travail**

Processes

process	le procédé	mechanisation	le machinisme
mass production	la production en grande série	assembly line	la chaîne de montage
automation	l'automation (*f.*)	electronics	l'électronique (*f.*)

Verbs

to sign on	engager	to set up, get going (*process, machine*)	mettre sur pied
to sack, lay off	congédier, renvoyer		
to strike	se mettre en grève	to incur (*expense*)	encourir
		to train (*apprentices*)	former
to earn one's living	gagner son pain		
		to slow down (*of production*)	(se) traîner, ralentir
to increase (*production*)	accroître		

Phrases

those everlasting wage claims	ces éternelles revendications
to get a good wage	toucher un bon salaire
with shirt-sleeves rolled up	en bras de chemise
the familiar din of the factory	le fracas familier de la fabrique
the rapid rhythm of the machines	le rythme précipité des machines
the Unions are asking for wage increases	les Syndicats réclament des majorations de salaires
2000 h.p.	une puissance de 2000 chevaux
to supply incentive	stimuler
to be seething with activity	grouiller d'activité
to work without human help	fonctionner sans intervention humaine
to get piece rates	être payé à la tâche
to have 1000 workers on the payroll	compter 1000 ouvriers
to manufacture on a large scale	fabriquer sur une grande échelle

ESSAYS

Visite à une exposition industrielle.
Les grèves sont-elles justifiées?
Notre avenir industriel.
Description d'une usine.
L'importance des syndicats.
Problèmes psychologiques de l'industrie moderne.

19. INTERNATIONAL RELATIONS—LES RELATIONS INTERNATIONALES

International Groupings

U.N.O.	l'O.N.U. (Organisation des Nations Unies)
Security Council	le Conseil de Sécurité
N.A.T.O.	l'O.T.A.N. (Organisation du Traité de l'Atlantique Nord)
S.E.A.T.O.	l'O.T.A.S.E. (Organisation du Traité de l'Asie du Sud-Est)

Atlantic Pact	le Pacte (L'Alliance) Atlantique
the West	l'Ouest (*m.*), les Occidentaux (*m.pl.*)
Council of Europe	le Conseil de l'Europe
Common Market	le Marché Commun
the Great Powers	les Grandes Puissances
the neutrals	les neutres (*m.*)
coloured peoples	les peuples (*m.pl.*) de couleur
Afro-Asian bloc	le bloc afro-asiatique
satellites	les satellites (*m.*)
puppet regime	le régime fantoche

Areas

the Middle East	le Moyen-Orient	West Berlin	Berlin-Ouest
the Far East	l'Extrême-Orient		

Cold War

the Cold War	la guerre froide	propaganda	la propagande
Iron Curtain	le rideau de fer	trouble spot	le point névralgique
co-existence	la coexistence	arms race	la course aux armements
tension	la tension	split	la scission
relaxation of tension	la détente		
balance of power	l'équilibre (*m.*)		
non-intervention	la non-intervention		

Diplomatic Exchanges

step	la démarche	a non-committal reply	une réponse qui n'engage à rien
note	la note	proposal	la proposition
talks	les pourparlers (*m.*)	text, statement	un énoncé
crisis	une crise		

Conferences

Summit Meeting	la Rencontre au Sommet	escape, escape clause	une échappatoire
programme	l'ordre (*m.*) du jour	hard bargaining	l'âpre marchandage (*m.*)
agreement	un accord	bluffing	le bluff
policy	la politique	blackmail	le chantage
clash	le heurt	compromise	le compromis
sabre-rattling	les menaces (*f.*) de guerre	guarantee	la garantie
settlement	la résolution (d'une question)		

Adjectives

hungry	affamé	unstable	instable
illiterate	illettré	protected (*of nations*)	sous tutelle
uncommitted	non aligné	unanimous	unanime
pro-Western	pro-occidental		

Verbs

to carry out (policy)	mener (une politique)
to lead to	aboutir à, entraîner
to guarantee (*independence*)	garantir
to bluff	bluffer
to veto	mettre son veto à
to conclude (a treaty)	conclure (un traité)
to break (an alliance)	rompre (une alliance)
to lay down (conditions)	poser, fixer (des conditions)
to woo (*countries*)	faire des avances à
to address (a note)	adresser (une note)
to be held (*a conference*)	se tenir
to achieve (agreement)	réaliser (un accord)
to deteriorate (*situation*)	empirer, s'aggraver
to envisage	envisager
to publish (a communiqué)	publier (un communiqué)
to intensify (*efforts, help*)	intensifier
to implement (*policy*)	mettre en œuvre
to originate (in)	avoir ses origines (dans)

Phrases

to carry out subversive activities	exercer une action subversive
interference in domestic affairs	l'immixtion dans les affaires intérieures
to show the velvet glove	faire patte de velours
to play for time	tâcher de gagner du temps
to say one thing and mean another	ne pas dire ce qu'on pense
to put pressure on	faire pression sur
to have serious repercussions	avoir de graves répercussions
to oppose strength with strength	opposer la force à la force
to increase one's watchfulness	redoubler de vigilance
to suffer from undernourishment	souffrir de sous-alimentation
to offer technical help	offrir une coopération technique
to help underdeveloped areas	porter aide aux régions sous-développées
to get self-determination	devenir indépendant
rising population	l'accroissement (*m.*) de la population
to proceed gradually	procéder par étapes
to come into force	entrer en vigueur
to observe strict neutrality	observer une stricte neutralité
to save one's face	sauver la face
to lose face	perdre la face
disarmament subject to international control	le désarmement soumis aux contrôles internationaux

ESSAYS

La guerre froide.

La coexistence.

Que faut-il faire pour avoir une paix durable?

Vers un gouvernement mondial.

L'O.N.U.

'La France n'est plus une puissance de troisième ordre.' Que pensez-vous de ce jugement?

See also 38. WAR.

20. LITERATURE—LA LITTÉRATURE

Books, Works

work	**une œuvre**	sequel	**la suite**
novel	**le roman**	collection	**le recueil**
short story	**le conte**	royalties	**les droits** (*m.*) **d'auteur**
long short story	**la nouvelle**		
narrative	**le récit**		

People

author	**un auteur; un écrivain** (*more general*)	short-story writer	**le conteur**
		essayist	**un essayiste**
		publisher	**un éditeur**
dramatist	**le dramaturge**	critic	**le critique**
novelist	**le romancier**		

Content

criticism	**la critique**	subject-matter	**le fond**
bias	**le parti-pris**	moral	**la morale**
environment	**le milieu**	picture (*of place, age*)	**le tableau**
plot	**une intrigue, une action**	illustration (*picture*)	**la gravure**
event	**un événement**	climax	**le point culminant**
ending	**le dénouement**		
character	**le personnage**	local colour	**la couleur locale**

Adjectives

dull, insipid	**fade**	unequal	**inégal**
improbable	**invraisemblable**	witty	**spirituel**
exciting	**palpitant, passionnant**	absorbing	**absorbant**
		fascinating	**fascinant**
commonplace	**banal**	first-class	**de premier ordre**
amusing	**divertissant**		

Verbs

to bring out, stress	**mettre en valeur (en lumière), faire ressortir**	to be entitled	**être intitulé**
		to deal with	**traiter de**
		to stand out	**se dégager**
to flip through	**feuilleter**	to thicken (*of plot*)	**se compliquer**
to depict	**dépeindre**	to point out	**signaler**
to appear (*of books*)	**paraître**		

Phrases

to be a bad judge of human nature	**juger mal la nature humaine**
since its appearance in 1880	**depuis sa parution en 1880**
he knows how to hold one's interest	**il sait soutenir l'intérêt**
the novel gets off to a slow start	**le roman démarre lentement**
its best feature is . . .	**ce qu'il a de meilleur, c'est...**
the story drags rather	**l'histoire traîne un peu**

the style leaves something to be desired	**le style laisse à désirer**
I like his plays	**ses pièces me plaisent**
as the story develops	**à mesure que l'histoire se déroule**
the author's aim is to show	**l'auteur a pour but, se propose, de montrer**
the book is a vehicle for his philosophy	**le livre sert de véhicule à sa philosophie**
his book fills a long-felt want	**son livre comble une lacune**
how can one fail to admire . . . ?	**comment ne pas admirer...?**
to say that he writes well would be superfluous	**dire qu'il écrit bien serait superflu**
that's not the least of its virtues	**ce n'est pas là son moindre mérite**
every reader will be grateful that he has said . . .	**tout lecteur lui saura gré d'avoir dit...**
to draw from life	**peindre sur le vif**
to come out in a paper-back	**paraître dans une collection de livres de poche, de livres brochés**

ESSAYS

Quel profit peut-on tirer de la lecture d'un roman?
Critique d'une œuvre que vous avez lue récemment.
Un chapitre de mon autobiographie.
Dites quelle espèce de livre vous préférez pour le simple plaisir de la lecture, et expliquez les motifs de ce plaisir.
Quel plaisir trouvez-vous à la poésie? Joue-t-elle un rôle important dans la vie quotidienne?
Si l'on vous offrait à lire un livre de contes de fées ou un roman d'aventures interplanétaires, lequel choisiriez-vous?
S'il ne devait rester, de toute l'œuvre de votre auteur préféré, qu'un seul livre, lequel conserveriez-vous? Pourquoi?
Votre bibliothèque idéale.
Quel profit avez-vous tiré de l'étude d'une littérature étrangère?
La fiction dépasse-t-elle la réalité?

21. MOTORING—L'AUTOMOBILISME (*m.*)

Roads and Surfaces

tarred road	**la route goudronnée**	bend	**le virage; le coude** (*sharp*)
cobbles	**le pavé**	hairpin bend	**le virage en épingle à cheveux**
motorway	**une autoroute**	crossroads	**le carrefour**

People

driver	**le chauffeur** (*private, also employed*); **l'automobiliste** (*m.*)	pedestrian	**le piéton**
		passenger	**le passager**
		road-hog	**le chauffard**
		garage proprietor	**le garagiste**
		garage hand	**le mécanicien**
road user	**un usager (de la route)**	speed cop	**le motard**
		hitch-hiker	**un auto-stoppeur**

Parts of Car

make	la marque	paint	la peinture
driving-mirror	le rétroviseur	carburettor	le carburateur
windscreen	le pare-brise	windscreen-wiper	un essuie-glace
dashboard	le tableau de bord	exhaust	l'échappement (*m.*)
bonnet	le capot		
clutch	un embrayage	front seat	le siège avant
brake	le frein	rear seat	la banquette arrière
accelerator	un accélérateur		
hand-brake	le frein à main	door handle	la poignée
engine	le moteur	safety belt	la ceinture de sécurité
radiator	le radiateur		
wing	une aile	tank	le réservoir
bumper	le pare-chocs	horn	le klaxon
hood	la capote	sliding roof	le toit ouvrant
spare wheel	la roue de secours	hub-cap	un enjoliveur
boot	le coffre	Motor Show	le Salon de l'Auto
coachwork	la carrosserie		
rear wheel	la roue arrière	petrol	l'essence (*f.*)
chassis	le châssis	oil consumption	la consommation d'huile
starter	le démarreur		
choke	le starter	driving licence	le permis de conduire

Vehicles

open touring-car	la torpédo	traffic	la circulation (routière)
sports car	la voiture grand sport	old crock, jalopy	la bagnole, la guimbarde
motor coach	un autocar		
lorry	le camion	scooter	le scooter
motor-bike	la motocyclette	saloon	la conduite intérieure

Traffic Aids

car park	le parking, le parc à autos	by-pass	la déviation
		cross-over, fly-over	le passage supérieur, le toboggan
Highway Code	le code de la route		
road safety	la prévention routière	roundabout	le rond-point
		ring road	le boulevard circulaire, périphérique
sign, notice	le panneau		
lights	les feux (*m.*)		
pedestrian crossing	le passage clouté	maximum speed	la vitesse limite
one way street	la rue à sens unique	road map	la carte routière
		dual carriageway	la route à double voie

Driving

starting	le démarrage	acceleration	la reprise, une accélération
slowing down	le ralenti		

Causes of Accidents

drunkenness	l'alcoolisme (*m.*)	collision	le tamponnement, la collision
tiredness	la fatigue		
steering defect	une direction défectueuse	skid	le dérapage
puncture	la crevaison	breakdown	la panne

Traffic Misfortunes

jam	**un embouteillage**	rush hours	**les heures (*f.*) de pointe**
congestion	**l'encombrement (*m.*)**		

Adjectives

slippery	**glissant**	bumpy	**cahoteux**
unhurt	**indemne**	convertible	**décapotable**
underground	**souterrain**	icy	**couvert de glace, verglacé**

Verbs

to start	**démarrer**	to collide	**entrer en collision**
to run over	**écraser**	to pump up	**gonfler**
to skid	**déraper; faire une embardée (*across the road*)**	to hit	**heurter**
to cross (*another car*)	**croiser**	to reverse (*trans.*)	**mettre en marche arrière**
to consume	**consommer**	to reverse (*intrans.*)	**faire marche arrière**
to break down	**tomber en panne**	to park	**parquer, garer**
to get going again	**dépanner**	to impose (a fine)	**infliger (une amende)**
to switch on the ignition	**mettre le contact**	to pass	**dépasser, doubler**
to switch off	**couper le contact**	to be thrown out	**être éjecté**
to brake	**freiner**	to go along, proceed	**filer**
to overturn	**capoter**	to hoot	**klaxonner**
to potter about (*with repairs, etc.*)	**bricoler**		

Phrases

the new and exciting 8 H.P. Ford	**la nouvelle et formidable 8 C.V. (chevaux-vapeur) Ford**
to fill up with Caltex	**faire le plein de Caltex**
to be in bottom gear	**être en première (vitesse)**
to get into third gear	**passer en troisième**
to find oneself in heavy traffic	**se trouver dans un trafic intense**
to go at full speed	**rouler à toute vitesse**
disregard of lights	**le non-respect de signaux**
suspension of driving licence	**le retrait de permis de conduire**
infringement of the Highway Code	**une infraction au code de la route**
more than 700 were killed	**plus de sept cents furent tués**
no parking!	**défense de stationner!**
to miss narrowly	**éviter de justesse**
to pull in to the kerb	**se ranger le long du trottoir**

ESSAYS

Un accident sur la Route Nationale.
L'automobile—ennemi public numéro un.
Mon père et sa bagnole.
A quelle cause attribuez-vous les accidents routiers, et quels remèdes proposez-vous?
Quels changements l'automobile a-t-elle apportés dans notre manière de vivre?

See also 37. TOWN.

22. MUSIC—LA MUSIQUE

Instruments

stringed instrument	un instrument à cordes	the wood-wind	les bois (*m.*)
		grand piano	le piano à queue
wind instrument	un instrument à vent	cello	le violoncelle
		violin	le violon
percussion instrument	un instrument à percussion	viola	un alto à cordes
		double bass	la contrebasse
the brass	les cuivres (*m.*)	horn	le cor

Voices

treble	le soprano; la soprano (*singer*)	baritone	le baryton
		mezzo-soprano	le mezzo (-soprano)
alto	le contralto		
tenor	le ténor	solo	le solo
bass	la basse	duet	le duo

Accessories

bow	un archet	piano stool	le tabouret (de piano)
key (*of piano*)	la touche		
lid (*of piano*)	le couvercle	stand	le pupitre à musique

People

accompanist	un accompagnateur	lady singer (*professional*)	la cantatrice
conductor	le chef d'orchestre	composer	le compositeur
		soloist	le soliste
singer	le chanteur, la chanteuse	choir	le chœur

Pieces of Music

overture	une ouverture	aria	une aria
score	la partition	chamber music	la musique de chambre
libretto	le livret		

Performance

diction	la diction	acoustics	l'acoustique (*f.*)
touch	le toucher	range	l'étendue (*f.*)
playing	le jeu	recital	le récital
rendering, performance	une interprétation, une exécution		

'Pop' Music

pop singer	le chanteur de concerts	punch, gusto, verve	le brio
jazz	le jazz	beat	le rythme
jive	le jive	tempo	la cadence
rock and roll	le rock 'n roll	ballad, lyric	la romance, le couplet
blues	le blues		

Radiograms and Gramophones

gramophone (*electric*)	un électrophone
recording	l'enregistrement (*m.*)
L.P. record	le disque longue durée, le (disque) 33 tours
single	le (disque) 45 tours
record-player	le tourne-disques
radiogram	le combiné-radio-phono
record collection	la discothèque
record-seller	le disquaire
record-changer	le changeur automatique
tone control	le réglage de la tonalité
speed control	le réglage de la vitesse
turntable	le plateau, la platiné
juke-box	le 'juke-box', le phono à sous
stylus	une aiguille (de phono)
tape recorder	le magnétophone

Adjectives

raucous	rauque
high-pitched	aigu, aiguë
deep	profond
high-brow	intellectuel
low-brow	philistin, terre à terre
shrill (of voice)	perçant, strident
sensual	sensuel
nasal	nasillard
faultless	impeccable

Verbs

to bawl	brailler, s'égosiller
to tune	accorder
to pedal	appuyer sur la pédale
to hum	fredonner
to whistle	siffler
to render, perform	exécuter
to plug in	brancher
to wind up	remonter
to strike up	entonner
to sing in tune	chanter juste
to sing out of tune	chanter faux
to conduct	diriger
to 'send'	transporter
to make a record	enregistrer un disque, faire un enregistrement
to put on (a record)	passer

Phrases

the conductor, resplendent in evening dress, mounted the rostrum	le chef d'orchestre, resplendissant dans son habit de soirée, gravit les degrés de l'estrade
to have twelve curtain calls	avoir douze rappels, être rappelé douze fois
to have a beautiful voice	avoir une belle voix
the story is a bit unrealistic	l'intrigue manque de réalisme
her lovely voice has packed the concert halls	sa belle voix a souvent fait salle comble
it's the only criticism of him that one could make	c'est la seule critique qu'on pourrait lui adresser
I'm allergic to jazz	je suis allergique au jazz
it's a popular tune of the moment	c'est une rengaine à la mode
this record netted him a million dollars	ce disque lui a rapporté un million de dollars

this record sold a million copies	ce disque s'est vendu à un million d'exemplaires
this craze for 'Hi-Fi'	la vogue de la haute fidélité
to build up a record library	se constituer une discothèque
to record on L.P.	enregistrer sur (un) 33 tours
to make a devil of a noise	faire un vacarme de tous les diables

ESSAYS

Une visite à l'opéra.
Un concert d'orchestre.
Pourquoi je préfère le jazz à la musique classique.
Mon tourne-disques
La musique moderne.
La musique populaire.

See also 36. THEATRE.

23. THE NAVY—LA MARINE DE GUERRE

Ships

warship	le vaisseau de guerre	liberty boat	la vedette (des permissionnaires)
submarine	le sous-marin	escort vessel	le navire d'escorte, un escorteur
minesweeper	le dragueur de mines	frigate	la frégate
destroyer	le contre-torpilleur, le destroyer	sloop	un aviso
cruiser	le croiseur	flagship	le vaisseau amiral
battleship	le cuirassé	squadron	une escadre
aircraft-carrier	le porte-avions	fleet	la flotte
gunboat	la canonnière	naval unit	une unité navale
torpedo tube	le tube lance-torpilles		

Naval Establishments

Admiralty	le Ministère de la Marine; 'l'Amirauté'	naval base	le port de guerre
		naval dockyard	le chantier naval

Naval Ranks

ordinary seaman	le matelot	sub-lieutenant	un enseigne de vaisseau
leading seaman	le quartier-maître	lieutenant	le lieutenant de vaisseau
bo'sun	le maître de manœuvre	lieutenant commander	le capitaine de corvette
petty officer	le second-maître	commander	le capitaine de frégate
warrant officer	le maître principal	admiral	un amiral
midshipman	un aspirant, le midship		

Officer Categories

naval engineer	un ingénieur mécanicien (de la marine)	submarine officer	un officier sous-marinier
paymaster officer	le commissaire	flag-lieutenant	un officier d'ordonnance
gunnery officer	le canonnier	Fleet Air Arm	l'Aéronavale (*f.*)

Parts of Warship

ward-room	le carré des officiers	torpedo tube	le tube lance-torpillo
quarter-deck	la plage arrière	powder magazine	la soute aux poudres
flight deck	le pont d'envol		
gun turret	la tourelle		

People

ratings	les matelots	survivor	le survivant
shipwrecked man	le naufragé	lower deck	le personnel non-officier
crew	un équipage		

Equipment

depth charge	la grenade sous-marine	gun	la pièce de bord, le canon
		binoculars	les jumelles (*f.*)

Clothing

duffel coat	le duffel-coat	bell-bottoms	le pantalon à pattes d'éléphant
cap	la casquette		
navy blue	le bleu marine		

Verbs

to sail	naviguer	to sink	couler, sombrer (*intrans.*); faire sombrer, envoyer au fond (*trans.*)
to man	armer	to be refitting	être en radoub
to hoist (flag)	hisser (le pavillon)	to engage (the enemy)	attaquer (l'ennemi)
to pick up	recueillir	to steer (*intrans.*)	faire route
to be missing	manquer, être disparu	to hit (a mine)	toucher (une mine)
to submerge	plonger, faire une plongée	to rejoin (one's ship)	rallier (son bord)
to surface	faire surface	to sight	repérer
to launch	lancer	to detect (*submarine*)	détecter
to manœuvre	manœuvrer		
to zigzag	zigzaguer		
to go down	couler, sombrer		

Phrases

to be in command of a sloop	commander un aviso
to mount twenty guns	être armé de vingt canons
to serve aboard a destroyer	servir à bord (d')un contre-torpilleur
to cruise under water	naviguer en plongée

Fighting

to sustain heavy losses	subir de lourdes pertes
adrift in an open boat	à la dérive dans une embarcation découverte
to be lost with all hands	périr corps et biens
to sail in convoy	naviguer en convoi
to sink by the bows	couler par l'avant
to open fire at long range	ouvrir le feu à longue portée
to fire a broadside (salvo)	tirer une bordée (une salve)
to belch fire and smoke	vomir flammes et fumée
forty of the crew are missing	quarante membres de l'équipage sont portés disparus
on the high seas	en pleine mer

ESSAYS

Un combat en mer.
Voudriez-vous être officier de marine? Donnez vos raisons.
La valeur, de nos jours, d'une flotte de guerre.

See also 34. SHIPS AND THE SEA.

24. OUTER SPACE—L'ESPACE SIDÉRAL

Devices

device, contraption	un engin	space-ship	le vaisseau spatial, un astronef
rocket	la fusée		
satellite	le satellite	artificial planet	la planète artificielle

Personnel

'boffin', back-room boy	le savant	space-man	un astronaute
guinea-pig	le cobaye	superman	le surhomme

Equipment

launching ramp (pad)	la rampe (la plateforme) de lancement	pressurised cabin	la cabine étanche, pressurisée
lift	un ascenseur	recording equipment	les appareils enregistreurs
scaffolding	l'échafaudage (*m.*)	fuel	le carburant
gantry	le chantier	stabiliser	un aileron de stabilisation
space-suit	le scaphandre	count-down	le compte à rebours, le compte (décompte) à zéro
wireless transmitter	le poste émetteur		

Travel

space travel	le voyage interplanétaire	range	la portée
conquest of space	la conquête du cosmos	landing on the moon	un alunissage

Data

scientific data	**les données (*f.*) scientifiques**	weather forecasts	**les prévisions (*f.*) météorologiques**
pressure	**la pression**	weightlessness	**l'apesanteur (*f.*)**

Verbs

to guide (by remote control)	**téléguider**	to pick up (*messages*)	**capter**
to launch	**lancer**	to refuel	**se ravitailler (en carburant)**
to circle the sun	**tourner autour du soleil**	to eject (a capsule)	**éjecter (une capsule)**
to send back (*data*)	**renvoyer**	to hit the moon	**percuter la lune**
to come back safely	**revenir sain et sauf**	to put into orbit	**placer en orbite (*f.*)**
		to relay (*signals*)	**relayer**

Phrases

to reach a height of . . .	**atteindre une hauteur de...**
to be 100 miles up	**se trouver à 100 milles d'altitude**
to get a man into space	**projeter un homme dans l'espace (*m.*)**
the monkeys were recovered safely	**les singes furent récupérés sains et saufs**
to collect a capsule in mid-air	**happer une capsule au passage dans l'espace (en plein ciel)**
it's one of the milestones in history	**c'est un événement historique**
the limits of human endurance	**les limites de l'endurance humaine**

ESSAYS

'Space travel is bilge.' Discutez.
Un voyage vers la lune.
'Il nous reste tant de choses à faire ici-bas, qu'il est fou d'essayer la conquête de l'espace.' Que pensez-vous de ce point de vue?
La valeur des voyages dans l'espace.

See also 3. AVIATION.

25. PAINTING—LA PEINTURE

Types

oil-painting	**la peinture à l'huile**	etching	**une eau-forte**
water-colour	**une aquarelle**	sketch	**une esquisse, une ébauche, le croquis**
drawing	**le dessin**		
crayon drawing	**le pastel**	print	**une estampe**
woodcut	**la gravure sur bois**	masterpiece	**le chef-d'œuvre**

Places

studio	**un atelier**	exhibition	**une exposition**
museum	**le musée**	gallery	**la galerie**

Accessories

brush	**le pinceau**	paint-box	**la boîte de couleurs**
easel	**le chevalet**	canvas	**la toile**

Content

landscape	**le paysage**	seascape	**la marine**

Parts of Picture

foreground	**le premier plan**	background	**l'arrière-plan (*m.*)** **le fond**

Good and Bad Points

colouring	**le coloris**	balance	**l'équilibre (*m.*)**
lighting	**l'éclairage (*m.*)**		

Art Criticisms

genius	**le génie**	model, pattern	**le modèle**
predecessor	**le devancier**	school	**une école**

Adjectives

dull	**mat**	vivid	**vif, éclatant**
glossy	**brillant**	lifelike	**vivant**

Verbs

to hang up	**accrocher**	to pose	**poser**
to be hanging	**pendre**	to clash with (*colours*)	**jurer avec**
to impress	**impressionner**		
to call to mind	**évoquer**	to harmonise with	**se marier avec**
to sit (for)	**servir de modèle (à)**		

Phrases

he's mad on painting (*i.e.*, he likes it better than his job)	**il fait de la peinture son violon d'Ingres**
he does a bit of painting	**il fait de la peinture**
he paints like Turner	**il peint à la manière de Turner**
a first-class portrait	**un portrait de premier ordre**
to paint from nature	**peindre d'après nature**
it has been valued at 10 million	**on l'a évalué à près de 10 millions**
it's an absolute daub	**c'est du barbouillage**
it means nothing to me	**ça ne me dit rien**

ESSAYS

Décrivez une peinture fameuse que vous connaissez.
Une visite à une galerie de peinture.

26. PASTIMES—LES PASSE-TEMPS (*m.*)

fencing	**l'escrime (*m.*)**	ball	**la bille**
foil	**le fleuret**	cannon	**le carambolage**
		cushion	**la bande**
billiards	**le billard**	pocket	**la blouse**
cue	**la queue**	to pot	**blouser**

pigeon-shooting	le tir aux pigeons (artificiels)
pigeon-fancying	la colombophilie
mountaineering	l'alpinisme (*m.*)
pot-holing	la spéléologie
driving	l'automobilisme (*m.*)
riding	l'équitation (*f.*)
wrestling	la lutte
winter sports	les sports (*m.*) d'hiver
skiing	le ski
tobogganing	la luge
walking	la marche (*sport*); les promenades (*f.*) (*strolls*)
golf	le golf
club	la crosse
links	le terrain de golf, le golf
scouting	le scoutisme
scout	le scout, le boy-scout
girl guide	la guide (de France); une éclaireuse (*in Britain*)
scoutmaster	le chef de troupe
skittles	le jeu de quilles; le bowling
skittle alley	le terrain de jeu de quilles; la piste de bowling
darts	les fléchettes (*f.*)
bowls	les boules (*f.*)
bowling green	le terrain de boules, le boulodrome
bowling match	la partie de boules
skating	le patinage
skate	le patin
skating rink	la piste de patinage, la patinoire; le skating (*indoor*)
horse-racing	la course de chevaux
racecourse	un hippodrome
race meeting	le concours hippique
flat race	la course de plat
steeplechase	la course d'obstacles, le steeple-chase
jockey	le jockey
bet	le pari
tote	le totalisateur
start	le départ
finish	l'arrivée (*f.*)
tapes	les rubans (*m.*)
winning post	le poteau d'arrivée
hunting	la chasse
fox-hunting	la chasse au renard
stag-hunting	la chasse à courre
pack	la meute de chiens
horn	le cor
game	le gibier
poacher	le braconnier
gun	le fusil de chasse
beater	le rabatteur
foxhound	le chien courant
to be at bay	être aux abois
fishing	la pêche
trout fishing	la pêche à la truite
fly fishing	la pêche à la mouche
rod	la canne à pêche
bait	l'amorce (*f.*)
hook	l'hameçon (*m.*)
camping	le camping
to put up a tent	monter, dresser, une tente
to share a tent	coucher à plusieurs
to catch a cold	prendre froid
water-skiing	le ski nautique
underwater exploration	l'exploration sous-marine
diving-suit	le scaphandre
diver	le plongeur, le scaphandrier (*with diving-suit*)
flippers	les palmes (*f.*)

snorkel	le masque
return to the surface	la remontée
to have good lungs	avoir les poumons solides
to remain submerged	rester immergé
dancing	la danse
dance-hall	le dancing
jazz band	le jazz-band (*pl.* jazz-bands)
crafts	les métiers (manuels)
pets	les animaux familiers
canary	le serin
budgerigar	la perruche
photography	la photographie
conjuring	la prestidigitation
conjuror	le prestidigitateur
to do tricks	faire des tours (de passe-passe)
indoor games	les jeux (*m.pl.*) de salon
chess	les échecs (*m.*)
chessboard	un échiquier
castle	la tour
knight	le cavalier
pawn	le pion
bishop	le fou
square	la case
to checkmate	mater, faire échec et mat
draughts	le jeu de dames
draughtboard	le damier
cards	le jeu de cartes
bridge	le bridge
whist	le whist
spades	le pique
diamonds	le carreau
hearts	le cœur
clubs	le trèfle
trump	un atout
ace	un as
jack	le valet
trick	la levée
rubber	la belle
to shuffle	battre
to cut	couper
to deal	donner
children's games	les jeux d'enfants
to play hide-and-seek	jouer à cache-cache
top	la toupie
lead soldier	le soldat de plomb
kite	le cerf-volant
hoop	le cerceau

Verbs

to relax	se délasser, se relaxer
to stay indoors	rester à la maison
to excel at	exceller à

Phrases

in my spare time	à mes moments perdus
to play badly	jouer comme un pied
to be a mere beginner	n'être qu'un(e) novice
to have a stroke of luck	avoir un coup de veine
everything went right for me	tout s'est bien passé pour moi
he gave me a good hiding	il m'a flanqué une bonne raclée
play will begin at 3 P.M.	la partie commencera à 3 heures

ESSAYS

Mon passe-temps favori.
La danse.
'Peut-on aimer la chasse et être ami des bêtes?'
'Les Anglais et leurs diverses façons de perdre leur temps.' Commentez.

See also 35. SPORT.

27. POLITICS—LA POLITIQUE

People

citizen	**le citoyen**	Home Secretary	**le Ministre de l'Intérieur**
M.P.	**le député** (*French*); **le parlementaire** (*British*)	Foreign Secretary	**le Ministre des Affaires Étrangères**
politician	**le politicien, l'homme politique**	Chancellor of the Exchequer	**le Ministre des Finances** (*French*); **le Chancelier de l'Échiquier** (*British*)
Prime Minister	**le Président du Conseil** (*French*); **le Premier Ministre** (*British*)	Speaker	**le Président**
		Civil Servant	**le fonctionnaire**
Minister of Labour	**le Ministre du Travail**	party leader	**le chef de parti** (*French*); **le leader** (*British*)
Minister of Education	**le Ministre de l'Éducation nationale**	Cabinet Minister	**le Ministre d'État**
		statesman	**un homme d'état**

Parliamentary Procedure

speech	**le discours**	meeting (*of Cabinet*)	**la réunion**
bill	**le projet de loi**	debate	**le débat**
sitting	**la séance**	referendum	**le référendum**

Groupings

State	**l'État** (*m.*)	Lower Chamber	**l'Assemblée nationale** (*French*); **la Chambre des Communes** (*British*)
party	**le parti**		
opposition	**l'opposition** (*f.*)		
ministry	**le ministère**		
Cabinet	**le Conseil des Ministres** (*French*); **le Cabinet** (*British*)	the Socialists	**les Travaillistes** (*British*), **les Socialistes** (*French*)
Upper Chamber	**le Sénat** (*French*); **la Chambre des Lords** (*British*)	the Tories	**les Conservateurs**
		the 'authorities'	**les pouvoirs** (*m.*)

Adjectives

bitter	**acharné**	stormy (*debate*)	**orageux, houleux**
rowdy	**tapageur**	deafening	**assourdissant**

Budget Problems

income	**le revenu**	unbalanced budget	**le budget déséquilibré**
expenditure	**la dépense**		

Election

seat	**le siège**	electoral campaign	**la campagne électorale**
election	**une élection**	polling booth	**le bureau de vote**
elector	**un électeur**	voting paper	**le bulletin de vote**
public opinion poll	**le sondage de l'opinion**	floating vote	**les voix (*f.*) des indépendants, des indécis**
constituency	**la circonscription**	deposit	**le cautionnement**
universal suffrage	**le suffrage universel**		

Verbs

to resign	**se démettre**	to elect	**élire**
to make (a speech)	**prononcer (un discours)**	to return (to Parliament, *trans.*)	**renvoyer**
to support (a motion)	**soutenir, appuyer (une motion)**	to preside over	**présider**
to reject	**rejeter**	to introduce (a bill)	**présenter, déposer (un projet de loi)**
to vote	**voter**	to pass (a law)	**voter (une loi)**
to settle (a problem)	**résoudre (un problème)**	to forfeit (deposit)	**perdre (son cautionnement)**
to meet	**se réunir, se rassembler**		

Phrases

he entered politics 40 years ago	**il entra dans la politique il y a quarante ans**
to go to the polls	**aller aux urnes**
to call on someone to speak	**donner la parole à quelqu'un**
to gain a small majority	**obtenir une faible majorité**
I'm giving my vote to the Tories	**je donne ma voix aux Conservateurs**
the usual crowd of unsolved problems	**la masse habituelle de problèmes en suspens**
to break one's word	**manquer à sa parole**
to put up as a candidate	**se porter candidat**

ESSAYS

Vous êtes candidat à une élection parlementaire. Rédigez votre programme électoral.
La politique en Angleterre.
Un Français à Westminster.
Une campagne électorale en Angleterre.
Votre plus grande ambition, est-ce de devenir homme politique?
La carrière du politicien.
La vie et la mort d'un politicien célèbre.
'Seuls les pessimistes font de la politique.' Discutez.
En qualité de Premier Ministre (ou de Ministre des Affaires Étrangères) vous prononcez à la radio un discours où vous exposez vos principes. Quels sont ces principes?

28. THE PRESS—LA PRESSE

Newspaper

daily	**le quotidien, le journal**
weekly	**l'hebdomadaire (*m.*)**
newsprint	**le papier de journal**

Newspaper Items

piece of news	**la nouvelle**
news	**les nouvelles**
cartoon	**le dessin**
strip-cartoon	**une histoire en bandes dessinées**
serial story	**le feuilleton**
sports report	**la chronique sportive**
book review	**la critique littéraire**
editorial	**un éditorial, un article de fond**
leader	**un article de tête**
small advertisements	**les petites annonces**
large advertisement	**la réclame**
picture	**l'illustration (*f.*), la photographie**
obituary notice	**le faire-part de décès**
crossword	**le mot croisé**
gossip	**les échos (*m.*)**
financial news	**la chronique financière**
News in Brief	**faits divers**
snapshot, shot	**un instantané**

Divisions

headline	**le titre; la manchette (*sensational*)**
column	**la colonne**
section (political, sporting, fashion, horse-racing)	**la rubrique (politique, sportive, de la mode, hippique)**

People

gossip-writer	**un échotier**
subscriber	**un abonné**
editor	**le rédacteur**
reporter	**le reporter**
photographer	**le photographe; le caméraman (*with cine-camera*)**
special correspondent	**un envoyé spécial**

Sales, etc.

News Agency	**une Agence d'Informations**
newspaper stall	**le kiosque**
newsvendor	**le vendeur de journaux**
newsagent	**le marchand de journaux**
censorship	**la censure**
copy	**un exemplaire**

Magazines

comic	**un journal amusant**
periodical	**la revue, le périodique**
magazine (*illustrated*)	**le magazine**

Magazine Features

picture	**la gravure**	dress pattern	**le patron**
love story	**une histoire d'amour**	beauty hints	**les conseils (*m.*) de beauté**
recipe	**la recette de cuisine**	glossy paper	**le papier brillant**

Adjectives

daring	**osé, audacieux**	sordid	**sordide**
bold	**tranchant**	trivial	**trivial, banal**
objective	**objectif**		

Verbs

to come out	**paraître**	to muzzle (the Press)	**museler (la presse)**
to subscribe to	**s'abonner à, être abonné à**		

Phrases

it's the mouthpiece of the Socialist party	**c'est le porte-parole du parti travailliste**
mass circulation paper	**un journal à grand tirage**
known for its excellent reporting	**connu pour ses excellents reportages**
to concentrate on sex and violence	**se spécialiser dans le sensuel et le violent**
to intrude on someone's grief	**venir troubler la douleur de quelqu'un**
to print 3 million copies	**tirer à 3 millions d'exemplaires**

ESSAYS

Mon journal favori.
La presse en Angleterre.
L'influence de la presse.
Quelles limites donneriez-vous à la liberté de la presse?
Mémoires d'un reporter.

29. RADIO AND TELEVISION—LA RADIO (T.S.F.) ET LA TÉLÉVISION

Equipment

1. *Radio*

set	**le poste, le récepteur**	aerial	**une antenne**
		valve	**la lampe**
transmitting set	**le poste d'émission; un émetteur (*portable*)**	loudspeaker	**le haut-parleur**
		battery	**la pile**
		accumulator	**un accumulateur**
		microphone	**le micro(phone)**
portable set	**le poste portatif**	point, plug	**la prise**
transistor	**le transistor**	dial	**le cadran**
knob	**le bouton**		

2. *T.V.*

T.V. set	**le téléviseur, l'appareil de télévision**	screen	**un écran**
		cathode-ray tube	**un tube à rayons cathodiques**

Services

broadcasting	**la radiodiffusion**	network	**le réseau**
broadcast	**une émission**	commercial T.V.	**la télévision commerciale**
good reception	**la bonne audition**	telerecording	**l'enregistrement (*m.*)**
poor picture	**une image défectueuse**	telefilm	**le film télévisé**
good picture	**une image nette**		
channel	**la chaîne**		

Physical Phenomena

atmospherics	**les parasites (*m.*)**	short wave	**les ondes courtes**
long wave	**les grandes ondes**	wave-length	**la longueur d'onde**
medium wave	**les ondes moyennes**	tuning	**le réglage**

People

announcer	**un speaker, un annonceur; une speakerine**	cameraman	le caméraman; **un opérateur (*in studio*)**
producer	**le producteur**	broadcaster	le chroniqueur (-euse), le speaker
viewer	**le téléspectateur**		
listener	**un auditeur**		
wireless fan	**le sans-filiste**	interviewer	**un interviewer**
moron	**un abruti**	disc-jockey	**le présentateur (des disques)**
comic	**le comique**		

Programmes

gramophone recital	**le récital de disques**	light music	**la musique légère**
dance record	**le disque de musique de danse**	sports report	**le commentaire (reportage) sportif**
weather forecast	**le bulletin météorologique, les prévisions (*f.pl.*) du temps**	interview	**une interview (avec une célébrité)**
news bulletin	**le bulletin d'actualités, le journal parlé**	schools programme	**l'émission (*f.*) scolaire**
newsreel, T.V. news	**le journal télévisé**	chamber music	**la musique de chambre**
serial	**le feuilleton**	'music while you work'	**'travaillez en musique'**
brains trust	**le brain-trust**	interval	**la pause**
quiz	**le jeu radiophonique**	performance	**la représentation**
children's hour	**l'heure (*f.*) des enfants**	instalment	**le numéro**
advertisement	**une réclame**	script	**le script, le texte**
variety	**les variétés (*f.*)**	time signal	**le signal horaire**
		magazine programme	**le magazine**

Adjectives

short-sighted	**myope**	harmful (*effect*)	**nocif, nuisible**

Verbs

to turn on	allumer *(le poste)*	to sponsor	**patronner**
to turn off	**fermer, éteindre** (*le poste*)	to view	**regarder**
		to listen in	**être à l'écoute**
to plug in	**brancher**	to tune in (to)	**régler (sur)**
to switch on (*electricity*)	allumer *(une lampe)*, mettre en marche	to turn up (the sound)	augmenter (le son)
to pick up (*station*)	**capter**	to advertise	**faire de la publicité**

Phrases

to tire one's eyes looking at the screen	**se fatiguer les yeux à regarder l'écran**
T.V. has changed the life of the man in the street	**la Télévision a transformé la vie du commun des mortels**
it's just a form of escape	**ce n'est qu'un moyen d'évasion**
to satisfy the need of relaxation	**satisfaire à un besoin de détente**
hours of passive viewing	**des heures de passivité**
a slave of the 'telly'	**un(e) esclave de la Télé**
to plug programmes with advertisements	**intercaler des réclames dans les émissions**
to attract as many viewers as possible	**attirer le maximum de téléspectateurs**

ESSAYS

La T.S.F. devant la concurrence de la Télévision.
La Télévision, ennemi public numéro un.
L'influence de la Télévision est-elle salutaire ou nuisible?
La Télévision décourage-t-elle la lecture?
Le rôle de la Télévision dans l'enseignement.
Êtes-vous pour ou contre la Télévision Commerciale?

30. RAILWAY—LE CHEMIN DE FER

Engine

diesel engine	**la locomotive diesel**	front	**l'avant (*m.*)**
		funnel	**la cheminée**
tender	**le tender**	smoke	**la fumée**
brake	**le frein**	underground train	**la rame (du Métro)**
buffer	**le tampon**		
whistle	**le sifflet**		

Train

compartment	le compartiment	guard's van	le fourgon de queue
corridor	le couloir		
luggage rack	**le filet**	W.C.	**le cabinet de toilette**
communication cord	**la sonnette d'alarme**	smoker	**le compartiment pour fumeurs, le 'fumeurs'**
window	**la glace**		
door	**la portière**		
communicating door	**la porte de communication**	non-smoker	**le 'non-fumeurs'**
		'concertina' (*passage between two coaches*)	**le soufflet**
sleeping car	**le wagon-lit**		
restaurant car	**le wagon-restaurant**		
seat (row of seats)	**la banquette**	rolling stock	**le matériel roulant**

Station

station	la gare; la station (*smaller station, also Underground*)	platform	le quai
		barrier	la barrière
		stairway	l'escalier (*m.*)
		cloakroom	la consigne
escalator	un escalier roulant	waiting room	la salle d'attente
		exit	la sortie
booking office	le guichet	refreshment room	le buffet
timetable	un horaire (*poster*); un indicateur (*book*)	bookstall	le kiosque
		subway	le passage souterrain

People

station-master	le chef de gare	plate-layer	un ouvrier de la voie
guard	le chef de train		
driver	le mécanicien	breakdown gang	une équipe de secours
stoker	le chauffeur		
inspector	le contrôleur	season-ticket holder	un abonné
porter	le porteur		
railwayman	le cheminot	rescuer	le sauveteur

Types of Train

express	le rapide	down train	le train montant
fast train	un express	up train	le train descendant
slow train	un omnibus		
goods train	le train de marchandises	excursion train	le train de plaisir
main line train	le train de grande ligne	passenger train	le convoi de voyageurs
workmen's train	le train ouvrier	diesel rail car	un autorail

Luggage

luggage	les bagages (*m.*)	trolley	le chariot
trunk	la malle	label	une étiquette
bag	le sac	luggage ticket	le bulletin (de bagages)
case	la valise		
package	le colis		

Journey

whistling, hissing	le sifflement	crash	la collision, le tamponnement
rocking, pitching	le tangage		
rolling	le roulis	derailment	le déraillement

Track

track	la voie	level-crossing	le passage à niveau
rail	le rail		
points	l'aiguillage (*m.*)	curve	la courbe
sleeper	la traverse	gauge	l'écartement (*m.*) de la voie
signal	le signal		
signal-box	la guérite à signaux	marshalling-yard	la gare de triage
		network	le réseau (ferroviaire)
cutting	le déblai, la tranchée	buffer	le butoir
embankment	le remblai	gradient	la rampe (*up*), la pente (*down*)

Tickets

single	**le billet simple**	workman's ticket	**la carte de travail**
return	**le billet aller et retour**	platform ticket	**le billet de quai**
season ticket	**la carte d'abonnement**	luggage ticket	**le bulletin de consigne**
cheap ticket	**le billet à prix réduit**		

Adjectives

grimy, sooty	**couvert de suie**	out-of-date	**périmé**
smoky	**enfumé**	unhurt	**indemne**
dreary	**triste, morne**		

Verbs

to puff	**haleter**	to register (*luggage*)	**enregistrer**
to accelerate	**accélérer**	to wave (*flag*)	**agiter**
to slow down	**ralentir**	to crash	**s'écraser**
to brake	**freiner**	to pile up	**s'entasser**
to start	**s'ébranler**	to start upon, tackle (a curve)	**amorcer (une courbe)**
to shunt	**manœuvrer, aiguiller**	to break (*journey*)	**interrompre**
to pick up	**prendre**	to come off the rails	**dérailler**
to set down	**déposer**		

Phrases

to arrive at the stated time	**arriver à l'heure prévue**
the signal is up (against us)	**le signal est fermé**
the signal is down	**le signal est ouvert**
the train thundered past	**le train passa avec un bruit de tonnerre**
the train was twenty minutes late	**le train avait un retard de vingt minutes**
a train coming from Manchester	**un train en provenance de Manchester**
45 m.p.h.	**75 km à l'heure**
is there a connection for . . . ?	**y a-t-il une correspondance pour ...?**
to rush (scorch) through the station at full speed	**brûler la gare à toute vapeur (vitesse)**
to get in the train	**monter en wagon, en voiture**
seat facing the engine	**une place dans le sens de la marche du train**
to sit with one's back to the engine	**être assis dans le sens contraire de la marche du train**
to look up a train	**consulter l'indicateur**
to turn on (off) the heating	**ouvrir (fermer) le chauffage**
how long do we stop?	**combien (de minutes) d'arrêt?**
to put on three (four) times the number of trains	**tripler (quadrupler) les trains**
to search among the wreckage	**fouiller parmi les décombres**
electrification is being slowly carried out	**l'électrification se poursuit lentement**
to increase speed without endangering safety	**augmenter la vitesse sans compromettre la sécurité**

ESSAYS

La journée d'un mécanicien.
Les chemins de fer britanniques.
Quelques progrès ferroviaires.
Quel est l'avenir du chemin de fer?
Un tamponnement (un déraillement).
Une aventure en chemin de fer.

31. RELIGION—LA RELIGION

Religious Occasions

Christmas	**Noël** (*m.*)	Good Friday	**Vendredi saint**
Easter	**Pâques** (*m.*)	Lent	**le Carême**
Whitsun	**la Pentecôte**	Palm Sunday	**le Dimanche des Rameaux**
Shrove Tuesday	**Mardi gras**		
Ash Wednesday	**Mercredi des cendres**		

Religions

Christianity	**le christianisme**	Mahommedanism	**l'islamisme** (*m.*)
Catholicism	**le catholicisme**	atheism	**l'athéisme** (*m.*)
Protestantism	**le protestantisme**		

Officials

priest	**le prêtre**	bishop	**un évêque**
curate, parish priest	**le curé**	archbishop	**un archevêque**
		pope	**le pape**
parson (*Protestant*)	**le pasteur**	sidesman	**le marguillier**

Other Persons

sinner	**le pécheur, la pécheresse**	choirboy	**un enfant de chœur, le chantre**
believer	**le croyant**		
Christian	**le chrétien**	chorister	**le choriste**
Jew	**le juif**	organist	**un organiste**
atheist	**un athée**	worshippers	**les fidèles** (*m.*)
martyr	**le martyr**	congregation	**l'assistance** (*f.*)
choir	**le chœur**		

Parts of Service

service	**un office** (*Catholic*); **le service, le culte** (*Protestant*)	psalm	**le psaume**
		children's address	**le catéchisme**
		prayer	**la prière**
		baptism	**le baptême**
mass	**la messe**	funeral	**les funérailles** (*f.pl.*)
communion	**la communion**		
preaching	**la prédication**	wedding (*in church*)	**le mariage religieux**
sermon	**le sermon**		
hymn	**une hymne**	wedding (*at register office*)	**le mariage civil**
anthem	**une antienne**		
chant	**la psalmodie**	organ recital	**le récital d'orgue**

Buildings

church	**une église**	pulpit	**la chaire**
cathedral	**la cathédrale**	lectern	**le lutrin**
chapel	**la chapelle**	choir stalls	**les stalles** (*f.pl.*)
abbey	**une abbaye**	parish	**la paroisse**
graveyard	**le cimetière**	bishopric	**un évêché**
pew	**le banc d'église**		

Essential Items

hymn book	le recueil de cantiques	collection plate	**le plateau**
		incense	**l'encens** (*m.*)
Bible	**la Bible**	organ	un orgue, (*f. au pluriel*-de grandes orgues)
prayer book	**le livre de messe, le paroissien**		
candle	**le cierge**	cross	**la croix**

Beliefs

faith	**la foi, la croyance**	God	**le bon Dieu**
		Christ	**Jésus-Christ**
hell	**l'enfer** (*m.*)	the Virgin Mary	**la Sainte Vierge**
heaven	**le ciel**	the Devil	**le Diable**
salvation	**le salut**	sin	**le péché**
purgatory	**le purgatoire**	Holy Ghost	**le Saint-Esprit**
angel	**un ange**		

Adjectives

holy	**saint**	tolerant	**tolérant**
pious	**pieux**	indifferent	**indifférent**
impious	**impie**	in Sunday-best	**endimanché**
irreligious	**irréligieux**	outworn	**périmé**
hypocritical	**hypocrite**	pagan, heathen	**païen**
immoral	**immoral**		

Verbs

to worship (*God*)	**adorer**	to take Mass	**célébrer la messe**
to sin	**pécher**	to attend Mass	assister à la messe
to baptise	**baptiser**	to confess	**confesser**
to practise (*a religion*)	**pratiquer**	to repent (of)	**se repentir (de)**
		to marry (a couple)	**marier (un couple)**
to pray	**prier**		
to bend the knee	**faire la génuflexion, s'agenouiller**	to bless	**bénir**
		to denounce	**dénoncer**
		to deal with	**traiter (de)**
to convert	**convertir**	to preach about	**faire un sermon sur...**
to believe (in)	**croire (en)**		

Phrases

to take up the collection	**faire la quête**
to sing out of tune	**chanter faux**
to sing in tune	**chanter juste**
to drone the prayers	**débiter les prières d'une voix monotone**
to read out the notices	lire les annonces de la semaine

to go into the dark interior	pénétrer dans le sombre intérieur
he's always been a regular church-goer	il a toujours été assidu aux offices
to go to Church willy-nilly	aller bon gré mal gré à l'église
they practise what they preach	ils prêchent d'exemple

ESSAYS

Un service religieux auquel j'ai assisté.
L'Angleterre, pays païen.
Mon église.
Un missionnaire célèbre.

See also 1. ARCHITECTURE.

32. SCIENCE—LA SCIENCE

People

technician	**le technicien**	physicist	**le physicien**
scientist	**le savant, l'homme de science**	chemist	**le chimiste**
		engineer	**un ingénieur**
		biologist	**le biologiste**

Sciences

chemistry	**la chimie**	cybernetics	**la cybernétique**
physics	**la physique**	genetics	**la génétique**
engineering	**la mécanique**	laboratory	**le laboratoire**
electronics	**l'électronique (*f.*)**		

The Mind

mind	**l'esprit (*m.*)**	discovery	**la découverte**
morals	**la moralité**	inventiveness	**l'esprit (*m.*) d'invention**
brain	**le cerveau**		
intellect	**l'intelligence (*f.*)**	technical progress	**le progrès technique**
research	**la recherche**		

Discoveries, Achievements

achievement	**la réalisation**	computer	**la machine à calculer, la calculatrice**
X-rays	**les rayons X (*m.*)**	penicillin	**la pénicilline**
electricity	**l'électricité (*f.*)**	flying	**le vol**
internal combustion engine	**le moteur à combustion interne**	space travel	**les voyages dans l'espace, interplanétaires**
descent to the ocean bed	descente au fond de de la mer en bathyscaphe	electronic brain	**le cerveau électronique**
anaesthetic	**un anésthésique**	vaccination	**la vaccination**
hydro-electric power	**l'énergie (*f.*) hydro-électrique**	inoculation	**l'inoculation (*f.*)**
atomic energy	**l'énergie (*f.*) atomique**	artificial insemination	**l'insémination artificielle**
splitting the atom	**la désintégration de l'atome (*m.*)**	colour television	**la télévision en couleurs**
radar	**le radar**	birth control	**la limitation des naissances, la conception dirigée**
automation	**l'automation (*f.*)**		
mechanical translator	**la machine à traduire**		

Evils

H-bomb	**la bombe H**	radio-active fall-out	**les retombées radioactives**
poison gas	**le gaz toxique**	genocide	**le génocide**
bacteriological warfare	**la guerre bactériologique**		

Evils to be Remedied

traffic accidents	**les accidents** (*m.*) **de la circulation**	refugees	**les réfugiés** (*m.pl.*)
		racialism	**le racisme**
		floods	**les inondations** (*f.*)
incurable illnesses	**les maladies** (*f.*) **incurables**	anti-semitism	**l'anti-sémitisme** (*m.*)
drought	**la sécheresse**	undernourishment	**la sous-alimentation**
smog	**le 'smog', la pollution atmosphérique**	illiteracy	**l'analphabétisme** (*m.*)
soil erosion	**l'érosion** (*f.*) **du sol**	noise	**le bruit**

Verbs

to save (labour)	**économiser (le travail)**	to perfect	**mettre au point**
		to poison	**empoisonner**
to test	**soumettre à un test**	to wipe out (*populations*)	**anéantir**
to experiment	**expérimenter**	to set off (fission)	**amorcer (la fission)**
to reason	**raisonner**		
to drive	**mener, faire marcher**	to tax (*powers*)	**mettre à l'épreuve**
		to popularise	**vulgariser**

Phrases

to improve the lot of human beings	**améliorer la condition humaine**
to alleviate human suffering	**alléger la souffrance humaine**
a remedy for T.B. (polio, cancer)	**un remède contre la tuberculose** (**la poliomyélite, le cancer**)
in the field of medicine	**dans le domaine de la médecine**
to lead a fuller life	**mener une vie plus large**
to help under-developed regions	**aider les pays sous-développés**
an increase in the output of energy	**un accroissement de la production d'énergie**
our mental progress outruns our moral development	**notre progrès mental va plus vite que notre développement moral**

ESSAYS

Les progrès des sciences, ont-ils créé un meilleur monde?
La vie et l'œuvre d'un(e) savant(e) éminent(e).
'Nous courons le risque de périr par nos propres inventions.' Discutez.
Dans le monde moderne, l'étudiant des sciences a une plus grande valeur que l'étudiant des humanités. Que pensez-vous de ce jugement?
Le savant a-t-il la responsabilité de faire un meilleur monde?
La journée d'un savant célèbre.
La bombe H.
Un savant français.
La découverte la plus importante de ce siècle.
Discutez les rapports entre l'homme de science et la société.
La vie en l'an 1984.

33. SEASIDE—LE BORD DE LA MER

Amusements

arcades	**les arcades (*f.*)**	maze	**le labyrinthe**
clock golf	**le jeu de 'clock-golf'**	swimming pool	**la piscine**
water-skiing	**le ski nautique**	bathing hut	**la cabine (de plage)**
slot machine	**le distributeur automatique**	pier	**la jetée**
fun fair	**le parc aux distractions, la foire**	shelter	**un abri**
		boarding house	**la pension**
		speedboat	**le loco-bord**
		sailing boat	**le voilier**

Persons

landlady	**la patronne, la propriétaire**	boarder	**le, la pensionnaire**
summer visitor	**un(e) estivant(e)**	old salt	**le loup de mer**
holiday-maker	**un vacancier, une vacancière**		

Geography

beach	**la plage**	rock pool	**la mare**
cliff	**la falaise**	high tide	**la marée haute**
sand-hill	**la dune**	low tide	**la marée basse**
sand	**le sable**	seaside resort	**la station balnéaire**
shingle	**les galets (*m.*)**		
breakwater	**le brise-lames**		

Clothes

beach robe	**le peignoir de bain**	shorts	**le short**
		rope shoes	**les espadrilles (*f.*)**
bathing costume	**le maillot**	bathing cap	**le bonnet de bain**
bathing trunks	**le caleçon de bain**	underwater goggles	**les lunettes sous-marines**
bikini	**le bikini**	flippers	**les palmes (*f.*)**
sun hat	**le chapeau de soleil**		

Accessories

sun-glasses	**les lunettes (*f.*) de soleil**	spade	**la bêche**
		pail, bucket	**le seau**
sun-tan oil (lotion)	**l'ambre (*m.*) solaire**	shrimping net	**le haveneau, la truble**

Denizens of the Sea

whelk	**le buccin**	crab	**le crabe**
shrimp	**la crevette**	lobster	**le homard**
cockle	**la clovisse, la coque**	jellyfish	**la méduse**
		seaweed	**les algues (*f.*)**
mussel	**la moule**		

Adjectives

balmy	**doux**	invigorating	**vivifiant**
salty	**salé**		

Verbs

to fleece, swindle	**tondre**	to dress	**s'habiller**
to paddle	**patauger, barboter**	to undress	**se déshabiller**
		to take a header	**piquer une tête**
to gambol	**gambader**	to get a tan	**brunir, bronzer**
to bathe	**se baigner**	to sun-bathe	**prendre un bain de soleil**
to stake (*at Casino*)	**miser**		

Phrases

to get a breath of fresh air	**prendre une bouffée d'air frais**
a tempestuous sea	**une mer en furie**
a howling gale	**une tempête furieuse**
dirty weather	**un sale temps, un temps de chien**
a heat-wave	**une vague de chaleur**
to hang about till lunch	**flâner jusqu'à l'heure du déjeuner**
to queue four abreast outside restaurants	**attendre devant les restaurants en colonnes par quatre**
people with transistors	**des gens armés de transistors**
there's nowhere to undress	**il n'y a pas d'endroit pour se déshabiller**
it's an absolute dump	**c'est un véritable trou**
to get the tips of your toes wet	**tremper le bout du pied**
to be sun-tanned	**avoir la peau brunie, tannée**
his skin's peeling	**il a la peau qui pèle**
to build sand-castles	**bâtir des châteaux de sable**
to get out of one's depth	**perdre pied**
to be carried away by the current	**être entraîné par le courant**
lovely sea trip!	**magnifique balade en mer!**
the sea's only a stone's throw from the boarding-house	**la mer n'est qu'à deux pas de la pension**
freshly painted boats	**les bateaux repeints à neuf**

ESSAYS

Une noyade (Death by drowning).
Une semaine à Blackpool.
Skegness ou St. Tropez?

See also 16. HOLIDAYS AND TRAVEL.

34. SHIPS AND THE SEA—LES BATEAUX (*m.*) ET LA MER

Types of Vessel

steamer	**le vapeur, le steamer; le paquebot** (*with mail and passengers*)	dinghy	**le youyou**
		barge, lighter	**le chaland, la péniche**
		ferry	**le bac**
		life-boat	**la baleinière, le canot de sauvetage**
Atlantic liner	**le transatlantique**		
cargo vessel	**le cargo**		
fishing boat	**le bateau de pêche**	tanker	**le pétrolier, le navire-citerne**
tug	**le remorqueur**	raft	**le radeau**
trawler	**le chalutier**	wreck	**une épave**
launch	**la chaloupe**		

Parts of Vessel

hull	**la coque**	fo'c'sle	**le gaillard d'avant**
bows	**l'avant (*m.*)**		
stern	**l'arrière (*m.*)**	alleyway	**la coursive**
stern-post	**un étambot**	rails	**le bastingage**
keel	**la quille**	flag	**le pavillon**
hatch	**le panneau; une écoutille (*hatchway*)**	bridge	**la passerelle (de commandement)**
hold	**la cale**	derrick	**le mât de charge**
propeller	**une hélice**	stabiliser	**le stabilisateur (de roulis)**
rudder	**le gouvernail**		
deck	**le pont**	engine	**la machine**
helm	**le barre**	boiler	**la chaudière**
gangway	**la passerelle (de service)**	plimsoll line	**la ligne de Plimsoll**

Parts of Liner

swimming pool	**la piscine**	port-hole	**le hublot**
dance floor	**la piste de danse**	deck chair	**le transatlantique**
smoking-room	**le fumoir**		
promenade deck	**le pont-promenade**	covered deck	**la promenade vitrée, le pont-abri**
cabin	**la cabine**		
bunk	**la couchette**		

In Harbour

landing-stage	**le débarcadère**	buoy	**la bouée**
crane	**la grue**	lighthouse	**le phare**
jetty, pier	**la jetée**	home port	**le port d'attache**

Discomforts

sea-sickness	**le mal de mer**	pitching	**le tangage**
rolling	**le roulis**		

People

sailor	**le marin**	purser	**le commissaire**
ship-owner	**un armateur**	pilot	**le pilote**
chief mate	**le second**	stevedore, docker	**le débardeur, le docker**
engineer	**le mécanicien**		
stoker	**le chauffeur**	survivor	**le survivant**
wireless operator	**le radio (de bord)**	castaway	**le naufragé**
officer of the watch	**un officier de quart**	stowaway	**le (passager) clandestin**

Appurtenances

jersey	**le chandail, le jersey**	compass	**la boussole**
life-belt	**la ceinture de sauvetage**	sou'wester (*hat*)	**le suroît**

Natural Features

coast	la côte (*from sea*); le rivage (*from land*); le littoral (*coast-line*)
iceberg	un iceberg
reef	le récif
cape	le cap

Sea

swell	la houle
wake, wash	le sillage
current	le courant
bottom, sea bed	le fond
wave	la vague, la lame; les flots (*m.*), waves (*poetic*)
spray	l'embrun (*m.*)
crest (*of wave*)	la crête
foam	l'écume (*f.*)

Weather

sea air	l'air marin
mist	la brume
squall	le grain

Adjectives

heavy (*sea, weather*)	gros
calm	calme
rough	agité
covered with foam (with white horses)	moutonneux
choppy	haché, clapoteux

Verbs

to go aground, founder	échouer
to sink	couler, sombrer
to anchor	mouiller
to go ashore	débarquer
to go on board	s'embarquer
to be wrecked	faire naufrage
to launch	lancer
to go under	enfoncer
to capsize	chavirer
to be drowned	se noyer
to weigh (cast) anchor	lever (jeter) l'ancre
to rise and fall	se balancer
to be sick	avoir le mal de mer
to collide with	aborder, entrer en collision avec
to call (at a port)	faire escale
to cross (the Atlantic)	traverser, faire la traversée de (l'Atlantique)
to coast	côtoyer, longer (*hug the shore*) faire le cabotage (*sail coastwise*)
to put into service	mettre en service
to lay down	mettre en chantier
to engulf, swallow up	engouffrer
to land	débarquer
to berth	s'amarrer
to ram	aborder, éperonner

Phrases

its cruising speed is 25 knots	sa vitesse de croisière est de 25 nœuds
it's an oil-burning vessel	ce vaisseau est chauffé au mazout
it's leaving for Buenos Aires	il est en partance pour Buenos Aires
it's not seaworthy	il n'est pas en état de naviguer

it's a veritable floating hotel	**c'est un véritable hôtel flottant**
to fly the French flag	**battre pavillon français**
tossed by the waves	**ballotté par les flots**
to brave the elements	**tenir tête aux éléments**
he was knocked down by a huge wave	**il fut renversé par un paquet de mer**
handed over to the will of wind and wave	**livré au caprice du vent et des vagues**
to be a good sailor	**avoir le pied marin**
to get engine trouble	**avoir une panne de machines**
man overboard!	**un homme à la mer!**
to be lost with all hands	**se perdre corps et biens**
to put to sea	**prendre le large**
to be off Cape Finistere	**être au large du Cap Finisterre**
to steer for Genoa	**mettre le cap sur Gênes**
to come alongside (*vessel*)	**accoster**
to take on fresh water	**prendre de l'eau douce**
she's got 2000 tons of diesel oil aboard	**il transporte 2000 tonnes de gas-oil**
to get a radio signal	**recevoir une communication par radio**

ESSAYS

Un naufrage.
Une croisière (A cruise).
Si un oncle riche vous offrait un voyage gratuit à New York, iriez-vous en avion ou en paquebot? Donnez vos raisons.

See also 23. NAVY.

35. SPORT—LE SPORT

Swimming	*La natation*
diving-board	**le tremplin**
deep end	le grand bain
swimming bath	**la piscine**
breast stroke, stroke	**la brasse**
side stroke	**la marinière**
crawl	**le crawl**
dive	**le plongeon**
to swim overarm	**nager à l'indienne**
to float	**faire la planche**
to dive	**plonger**

Boxing	*La boxe*
heavy-weight	**le poids lourd**
light-weight	**le poids léger**
bantam-weight	**le poids coq**
feather-weight	**le poids plume**
fly-weight	**le poids mouche**
punch	**le punch**
knock-out	**le knock-out**
round	**le round**
ropes	**les cordes** (*f.*)
ring	**le ring**
sawdust	**la sciure**
boxer	**le boxeur**
referee	**un arbitre**
weigh-in	**la pesée**
to throw in the towel	**jeter l'éponge**
he was knocked out	**il a été mis knock-out**
victory on points	**la victoire aux points**
he got a black eye	**il a eu l'œil au beurre noir**
to stagger back to one's corner	**retourner vers son coin en titubant**

to be down for the count	**rester sur le plancher pour le compte**
the bell went	**le gong a résonné**
Athletics	***L'athlétisme (m.)***
sprint	**la course de vitesse, le sprint**
hundred metre hurdles	**le cent mètres haies**
long distance race	**la course de fond**
relay race	**la course de relais**
obstacle race	**la course d'obstacles**
javelin	**le javelot**
discus	**le disque**
high jump	**le saut en hauteur**
pole jump	**le saut à la perche**
long jump	**le saut en longueur**
tug of war	**le tir à la corde**
track	**la piste**
lane	**le couloir**
tape	**la bande d'arrivée**
stop watch	**le chronomètre**
athlete	**un athlète**
runner	**le coureur**
jumper	**le sauteur**
to sprint	**faire un sprint**
to put the weight	**lancer le poids**
to clear the bar	**franchir la barre**
Tennis	***Le tennis***
forehand	**le coup droit**
backhand	**le revers**
drive	**le drive**
smash	**le smash**
cannonball service	**le service canon**
volley	**la volée**
rally	**la passe de jeu**
men's singles	**le simple-messieurs**
men's doubles	**le double-messieurs**
ladies' doubles	**le double-dames**
mixed doubles	**le double-mixte**
court	**le court, le terrain de tennis**
stop netting	**l'entourage (*m.*)**
net	**le filet**
in the 'tramlines'	**dans le couloir**
base line	**la ligne de fond**
whites	**la tenue blanche**
love	**zéro**
deuce	**égalité**
van in (out)	**avantage dedans (dehors)**
love game	**jeu blanc**
foot fault	**la faute de pied**
net!	**net!**
double fault	**double faute**
point	**le point**
Davis Cup	**la Coupe Davis**
tennis player	**le tennisman**
champion	**un as**
to hoist a lob	**faire (hisser) un lob, lober**
to knock up	**faire des balles**
to return	**renvoyer**
to put out (*ball*)	**envoyer hors jeu**
to go up to the net	**monter au filet**
to be in form	**être en forme**
to win the match	**gagner la partie**
Golf	***Le golf***
club	**la crosse de golf**
links	**le terrain de golf**
to drive	**jouer une crossée**
to hole out	**poter**
Rowing	***Le canotage, le rowing, l'aviron (m.)***
regatta	**la régate**
boat race	**la course de bateaux**
cox	**le barreur**
stroke	**le chef de nage**
bow	**le nageur de tête**
winning post	**le poteau d'arrivée**
to win by a canvas	**gagner par une épaisseur de toile**

General Terms

semi-final	la demi-finale	winner	le gagnant
final	la finale	fan	le fervent
round	le round, la reprise, la manche	official	un officiel
meeting (*sporting*)	le meeting	record holder	le recordman (*pl.* les recordmen)
Cup	la coupe	title holder	le détenteur du titre
championship	le championnat		
lap	une étape		
heat	une éliminatoire	team spirit	l'esprit (*m.*) d'équipe
opponent	un adversaire		
supporter	le supporter	well-matched	équilibré
trainer, coach	un entraîneur		

Verbs

to go in for (a sport)	pratiquer (un sport)
to cover (*distance*)	couvrir
to train (*intrans.*)	s'entraîner
to give oneself up to	s'adonner à
to sign (autographs)	signer (des autographes)

Phrases

what's the score?	quel est le score?
to beat the record held by X	battre le record détenu par X
professionalism is not common in that game	dans ce sport, le professionnalisme n'est pas répandu
to put up an excellent performance	réaliser une belle performance
to hold one's own with the best	rivaliser avec les meilleurs
to prefer brains to brawn	préférer le cerveau aux muscles
to come in well ahead	arriver largement en tête
to beat the record by a tenth of a second	battre le record d'un dixième de seconde
to be handsomely beaten	être largement battu
he's a real sportsman	c'est un beau joueur; c'est un sportsman, un sportif
to lose narrowly	perdre de justesse

ESSAYS

Le professionnalisme dans les sports—est-il bon ou mauvais?
'Notre amour du sport nous rend tout à fait ridicules.' Discutez.
Les grands concours internationaux, tels que les Jeux Olympiques, favorisent-ils l'amitié entre les peuples?
Mon sport favori.
'Le sport n'est qu'une méthode frivole de gaspiller le temps.' Discutez.
Un match passionnant auquel vous avez participé (ou que vous avez vu).
La pratique des sports, doit-elle être obligatoire dans les écoles?
Un exploit remarquable dans les annales du sport.

See also 26. PASTIMES.

36. THEATRE—LE THÉÂTRE

Parts of Theatre

stage	**la scène**
safety curtain	**le rideau de fer**
scenery	**le décor**
footlights	**la rampe**
wings	**les coulisses (*f.*)**
auditorium, house	**la salle**
pit	**le parterre**
stall	**le fauteuil d'orchestre**
gallery	**le paradis, le poulailler**
box	**la loge**
circle	**le balcon**
cloakroom	**le vestiaire**
dust sheet	**la bâche**
box-office (window)	**le guichet**
lobby	**le foyer**
poster	**une affiche**

Persons

attendant	**une ouvreuse**
producer	**le metteur-en-scène**
audience	**le public**
prompter	**le souffleur**
repertory company	**la troupe à demeure**
cast	**la distribution**
stage manager	**le régisseur**
theatre-goer	**un habitué**
dramatist	**le dramaturge**
critic	**le critique**
juvenile lead	**le jeune premier**

Performance

acting	**le jeu**
play	**la pièce (de théâtre)**
plot	**une intrigue**
character	**le personnage**
part	**le rôle**
rehearsal	**la répétition**
performance	**la représentation**
applause	**les applaudissements (*m.*)**
job, engagement	**un engagement**
interval	**un entr'acte**
review, criticism	**la critique**
first night	**la première**
curtain raiser	**le lever de rideau**

Adjectives

exciting	**palpitant, passionnant**
boring	**ennuyeux**
trite	**banal**
amusing	**divertissant**

Verbs

to clap	**battre des mains, applaudir**
to hiss	**siffler**
to fail	**échouer, faire un four**
to boo	**huer**
to book (*seat*)	**louer**
to make up	**maquiller**
to rehearse	**répéter**
to subsidise	**subventionner**
to take off, withdraw	**retirer**
to put on (*play*)	**monter**
to slate, pan, tear to shreds (*of critics*)	**éreinter**

Phrases

to go on the stage	faire du théâtre
to turn professional	passer professionnel
to sound curtain-up	frapper les trois coups
he always plays Julius Caesar	il joue toujours Jules César
she's on tour	elle est en tournée
to have a role worthy of one's talents	avoir un rôle à sa taille
to have a resounding success	avoir un succès retentissant
full house	salle comble
to be in evening dress	être en tenue de soirée (en frac)
to book seats in advance	louer les places d'avance
she acts with great skill	elle joue avec beaucoup de talent
there'll be a heavy demand for seats	les places seront très demandées (courues)
standing room only	places debout
the play didn't get across	la pièce n'a pas passé la rampe
the curtain rises at 8 sharp	on lève le rideau à huit heures précises
to post house-full notices	afficher 'complet'

ESSAYS

Une visite au théâtre.
Êtes-vous pour, ou contre, un Théâtre National?
Comparez une pièce française que vous connaissez bien avec une pièce anglaise traitant un sujet analogue.
Critique imaginaire, dans un journal, de la première d'une pièce française célèbre.
'Le but du théâtre est d'instruire, celui du cinéma est de divertir.' Discutez.

See also 4. CINEMA.

37. TOWN—LA VILLE

Parts of Town

suburbs	la banlieue; les faubourgs (*less respectable*)	circumference	le périmètre
		dormitory suburb	la banlieue-dortoir
district	le quartier	housing estate	la cité

Town Features

main square	la grand-place	swimming bath (open air)	la piscine en plein air
circus (*at road intersection*)	le rond-point	bandstand	le kiosque à musique
skyscraper	le gratte-ciel (*pl.* les gratte-ciel)	flower bed	le parterre
		car park	le parking, le parc à autos
Town Hall	l'Hôtel (*m.*) de Ville	landing strip	la piste d'atterrissage
department stores	les grands magasins	shopping centre	le centre commercial
park	le jardin public		
playground	le terrain de jeu	illuminated sign	la réclame lumineuse
block of flats	un immeuble		
bus station	la gare routière		

Persons

architect	**un architecte**	city-dweller	**le citadin**
town-planner	**un urbaniste**	commuter	**un(e) abonné(e), celui qui fait la navette**
pedestrian	**le piéton**	Town Councillor	**le Conseiller municipal**
motorist	**un automobiliste**		

Materials

materials	**les matériaux** (*m.pl.*)	aluminium	**l'aluminium** (*m.*)
		glass	**le verre**
concrete (reinforced)	**le béton (armé)**	steel	**l'acier** (*m.*)
		asphalt	**l'asphalte** (*m.*)

Drawbacks

alley	**la ruelle**	ribbon development	**l'extension** (*f.*) **linéaire**
slums	**les taudis** (*m.pl.*)	built-up areas	**les agglomérations** (*f.*)
slum area	**le bas quartier**	soot	**la suie**
waste ground	**le terrain vague**	pneumatic drill	**le marteau pneumatique**
hoarding	**le panneau d'affichage**	liquid efflux	**les eaux** (*f.pl.*) **d'égout** (*m.*)
scaffolding	**l'échafaudage** (*m.*)	traffic jam	**un embouteillage**
advertisement	**la réclame**	polluted air	**l'air vicié (pollué)**
exhaust fumes	**les vapeurs** (*f.*) **d'essence; les gaz** (*m.pl.*) **d'échappement** (*m.*)	poisonous fumes	**les fumées toxiques**

Aesthetic Qualities

symmetry	**la symétrie**	lack of proportion	**la disproportion**
mixture of styles	**le mélange de styles**	arrangement	**la disposition**
planlessness	**le manque de plan**		

Amenities

town planning	**l'aménagement** (*m.*) **des villes, l'urbanisme** (*m.*)	smokeless zone	**la zone sans fumées**
by-pass	**la déviation**	one-way street	**la rue à sens unique**
ring-road	**le boulevard circulaire, périphérique**	roundabout	**le rond-point, le carrefour à sens giratoire**
slum clearance	**la suppression des taudis**	fly-over	**le passage supérieur, le toboggan**
green belt	**la ceinture verte**	underpass	**le passage souterrain**
open spaces	**les espaces verts**		

Adjectives

tasteless	sans goût	teeming, swarming	grouillant
tortuous	tortueux	noisy	bruyant
residential	résidentiel	sprawling	étalé
unhealthy	malsain	heavy (*traffic*)	intense
busy (*of streets*)	animé		

Verbs

to put up	ériger, élever	to cover with smoke	enfumer
to by-pass	contourner	to dirty	souiller
to clash	jurer	to beautify	embellir
to bring out, show up	mettre en valeur	to date (from)	dater (de)
to sprawl	s'étaler	to radiate	rayonner
to harmonise (with)	se marier, s'harmoniser (avec)	to connect (*two parts of a town*)	relier
to clean up	faire le nettoyage	to commute	faire le va-et-vient, voyager avec un abonnement

Phrases

to lay out sports grounds	aménager des terrains de sport
to have 300,000 inhabitants	compter trois cent mille habitants
he has gone to live there	il y a élu domicile
the population is going up by 500 each month	la population s'accroît de 500 par mois
to have easy access to shops	être à portée des magasins
to lack communal activities	manquer d'activités sociales

ESSAYS

Une ville de l'avenir.
Ma ville idéale.
Ma ville.
Les horreurs de la vie urbaine.

38. WAR—LA GUERRE

Modern Weapons

conventional weapons	les armes conventionnelles, classiques	poison gas	le gaz toxique
rocket	la fusée	explosive charge	la charge explosive
rocket with nuclear warhead	la fusée à tête nucléaire	launching pad	la rampe de lancement
nuclear submarine	le sous-marin nucléaire	nuclear test	un essai (une expérience) nucléaire
Polaris missile	la fusée Polaris	operational base	la base (d'opérations)
long-range missile	le missile à longue portée	target	la cible
H-bomb	la bombe H (bombe à hydrogène)		

Effects of Modern War

radiation	**la radiation**	radio-active dust	**la poussière radio-active**
blast	**le souffle**	burns	**les brûlures** (*f.pl.*)
radio-active fall-out	**les retombées radio-actives, les déchets radio-actifs**	survival	**la survie**
		rubble	**les décombres** (*m.*)

Defence

Geiger counter	**le compteur Geiger**	underground shelter	**un abri souterrain**
radar screen	**un écran de radar**		

War and Politics

causes of war	**les causes de la guerre**	deterrent effect	**l'effet de dissuasion**
hostilities	**les hostilités** (*f.*)	a ban (on tests)	**une interdiction (des essais)**
call-up	**l'appel (sous les drapeaux)** (*m.*)	exchanges of information	**les échanges** (*m.*) **d'informations**
arms race	**la course aux armements**		
striking power	**la force de frappe**		

Persons

aggressor	**un agresseur**	casualties	**les morts et les blessés** (*m.pl.*)
spy	**un espion**		
War Minister	**le Ministre de la Guerre**	hostage	**un otage**
		brass-hat	**un officier d'état-major**
arms manufacturer	**le fabricant d'armes**	rebel	**un insurgé**

Adjectives

neutral	**neutre**	bacteriological	**bactériologique**
uncommitted	**non engagé**	devastating	**dévastateur**
harmful	**nocif**	supersonic	**supersonique**
war-mongering	**belliqueux**		

Verbs

to start (a war)	**déclencher (une guerre)**	to stockpile	**constituer des réserves**
to fight (a battle)	**livrer (une bataille)**	to rage (*of war*)	**sévir, faire rage**
		to issue (an ultimatum)	**lancer (un ultimatum)**
to intervene	**intervenir**		
to declare (war)	**déclarer (la guerre)**	to explode (a bomb)	**faire exploser (une bombe)**
to provoke	**provoquer**	to rain down upon	**s'abattre sur**
to break out (*of war*)	**éclater**	to diminish (tension)	**diminuer (la tension)**

to commit an act of aggression	**se livrer à une agression**	to liquidate	**liquider**
to carry out (reprisals)	**exercer (des représailles, *f.pl.*)**	to contaminate	**contaminer**
		to ban (*a bomb*)	**proscrire, interdire**
to detect (*explosion, radiation*)	**détecter, déceler**	to test	**tester, éprouver examiner**

Phrases

by all means short of war	**par tous les moyens à l'exclusion de la guerre**
to observe a strict neutrality	**observer une stricte neutralité**
to do great damage	**faire de grands dégâts**
to be inaccurate (*of guns*)	**manquer de précision**
radar stations will give warning of the attack	**les postes de radar vont déceler l'attaque**
to increase the desire for peace	**accroître le désir de paix**
to sign a surrender document	**signer l'acte de reddition**
hopes of speedy victory	**l'espoir d'une victoire rapide**
to wave the olive branch	**brandir le rameau d'olivier**
we're at war with the Russians	**nous sommes en conflit avec les Russes**
busy perfecting their weapons	**occupés à mettre leurs armes au point**
to live in fear of another war	**vivre dans la peur d'une nouvelle guerre**
to be on a war footing	**être sur le pied de guerre**
to have an effective range of 1000 km.	**avoir un rayon d'action de 1000 km**
to inflict heavy losses	**infliger de lourdes pertes**
to carry out a scorched earth policy	**pratiquer la tactique de la terre brûlée**
to give four minutes' warning	**donner quatre minutes d'avertissement, de préavis**

ESSAYS

Les conséquences d'une nouvelle guerre.
La guerre ancienne et la guerre moderne.

See also 2. ARMY; 3. AVIATION; 15. INTERNATIONAL RELATIONS; 23 NAVY.

2. ADDITIONAL PHRASES

(OF PARTICULAR VALUE FOR ABSTRACT SUBJECTS)

Comment

Nowadays no-one thinks such a thing	**De nos jours, personne ne pense chose pareille**
It's a very difficult question to answer	**C'est une question fort difficile à résoudre**
But there is another side to the question	**Mais il y a le revers de la médaille**
I agree with this opinion	**Je suis d'accord sur ce point**
Let us assume that this is so	**Mettons qu'il en soit ainsi**
I doubt whether this is so	**Je doute que ce soit vrai**
But it is not so	**Mais il n'en est pas ainsi**
The following are the factors that have to be reckoned with	**Voici les facteurs qui entrent en ligne de compte**
But here again one must be careful	**Mais ici encore il faut se méfier**
The situation admittedly leaves much to be desired	**La situation, de l'aveu général, laisse beaucoup à désirer**
This theory does not hold water	**Cette théorie ne tient pas debout**
One must weigh the pros and cons	**Il faut peser le pour et le contre**
There are plenty of people who think so	**Il y a bon nombre de gens qui sont de cet avis**
Such a view is hardly warranted	**Il serait abusif de le prétendre**
I don't think much of this argument	**De cet argument je fais peu de cas**
By its very nature such an argument is false	**De par sa nature même, un tel argument est faux**
Nothing can make me believe it	**Rien ne saurait me le faire croire**
I shall go thoroughly into the question	**Je vais approfondir la question**
This remark is not to the point (is irrelevant)	**Cette observation manque d'à-propos**
People attach much importance to this theory	**On attache beaucoup d'importance à cette théorie**
If we examine the question more closely, we shall see the facts in a different light	**Si nous examinons la question de plus près nous verrons les faits sous un jour différent**
Frankly, I don't believe it	**Franchement, je n'y crois pas**
By way of example, let us quote Winston Churchill	**A titre d'exemple, citons Winston Churchill**
Let us glance at this point of view	**Considérons brièvement ce point de vue**
Let us suppose they are right	**Supposons (supposé) qu'ils aient raison**
This is one of the questions of the hour	**C'est une des questions à l'ordre du jour**

Linkages

furthermore, moreover	**qui plus est; par-dessus le marché au surplus; du reste**
in a sense	**dans un sens**
however that may be	**quoi qu'il en soit**
after due consideration	**toute réflexion faite**

truth to tell	**à vrai dire, à la vérité**
and rightly so	**et pour cause; à bon droit; à juste titre**
it's the same with	**il en est de même de**
first of all	**tout d'abord**
in theory	**en théorie; théoriquement**
in large measure	**dans une large mesure**
without doubt	**sans aucun (nul) doute; à n'en pas douter**
in a word, in short	**en résumé; bref**
on the other hand	**en revanche; par contre**
and, strange to say . . .	**et, chose curieuse,...**
in principle	**en principe**
far from it	**loin de là**
in my opinion	**à mon avis**
apparently	**apparemment; à ce qu'il paraît; semble-t-il; paraît-il**
in point of fact	**par le fait, en fait**
in this respect	**à cet égard**
so that, and so	**si bien que (+ *Indicative*)**
in many respects	**à beaucoup d'égards**
in every respect	**à tous les égards**
at first sight	**à première vue**
let it not be thought that . . .	**qu'on n'aille pas croire que...**
in one way or another	**de façon ou d'autre; d'une manière ou d'une autre**
in other words	**en d'autres termes**
certainly, if you like	**si l'on veut**
need one add that . . . ?	**est-il besoin d'ajouter que...?**
in particular	**notamment**
all the more (because)	**d'autant plus (que)**
in any case	**de toute façon, en tout cas**
hence	**de là**
the fact remains that . . .	**toujours est-il que...**
it's still true to say that . . .	**on peut encore dire que...**
naturally	**bien entendu**
it's a surprising fact that . . .	**fait surprenant, c'est que...**
let's admit that . . .	**mettons (admettons) que...**
by general admission	**de l'aveu général**
whether we like it or not	**qu'on le veuille ou non**
a point to be borne in mind is . . .	**chose à retenir, c'est que...**
it's to be noted that . . .	**il est à noter que...**
some say that . . .	**d'aucuns prétendent que...**
one is tempted to conclude that . . .	**on est tenté de conclure que...**
to such an extent that . . .	**à tel point que...**
while admitting that . . .	**tout en admettant que...**
all in all	**à tout prendre; en fin de compte tout compte fait**
according to all the evidence	**de toute évidence**
in all probability	**selon toutes probabilités**
in other words	**en d'autres termes; autrement dit**
on all these heads	**sur tous ces chapitres**
setting this argument aside	**cet argument mis de côté**
all the same	**tout de même; n'empêche que (+ *Indicative*)**

to believe such people	**à en croire de telles gens**
taking this into account	**compte tenu de ceci**
or, better still	**ou, mieux encore (qui mieux est)**
it's doubtful whether . . .	**on peut se demander si...**
but, one may say, . . .	**mais, dira-t-on,...**
it can be objected that . . .	**on objectera que...**
on that point	**là-dessus**
in its turn	**à son tour**
the annoying thing is	**l'embêtant, c'est que...**
true	**il est vrai**
to quote	**au dire de**
as far as one can judge	**autant qu'on puisse en juger**
by and large, on the whole	**à tout prendre**
it's tantamount to saying, one might as well say	**autant dire que**
just as, in the same way as	**de même (que,** *before clause***)**
by a paradox	**de façon paradoxale**
on some points	**sur certains points**
even more, how much the more	**à plus forte raison**
it's a reason for believing	**c'est une raison de croire**
it would be an exaggeration to say	**il serait exagéré de dire**
in other circumstances	**en d'autres circonstances**
on the one hand . . . on the other	**d'une part... d'autre part**
basically	**dans le fond, au fond**

SOME ABSTRACT SUBJECTS

'L'union fait la force.'
Dans le monde moderne, il est impossible de dire toujours la vérité.
'Nous sommes responsables d'à peu près tous les maux dont nous souffrons.'
'L'argent est la source de tous les maux.'
Peut-on parler d'un caractère national?
'We would do well to attend to the French; we are so unlike them.'
Le dimanche anglais.
Lequel est le plus important: parler, lire, ou écrire une langue étrangère?
Les hommes et les femmes devraient-ils recevoir le même salaire?
Le patriotisme.
'Les gens heureux n'ont pas d'histoire.'
Le bien et le mal dans la vie de nos jours.
'Du sublime au ridicule il n'y a qu'un pas.'
Le bonheur.
Dans quel sens peut-on dire que tous les hommes sont égaux?
Il faut lire les auteurs plutôt que les critiques.
'Le sabre est toujours battu par l'esprit.'
La propagande.
La personnalité.
Le pessimisme.
Les superstitions populaires.
'A quelque chose malheur est bon.' (It's an ill wind that blows no-one any good.)
'Un point à temps en épargne cent.' (A stitch in time saves nine.)
La cuisine anglaise. (English cooking.)
Ce n'est pas dans la nouveauté, c'est dans l'habitude, que nous trouvons les plus grands plaisirs.
Faut-il toujours dire la vérité aux malades?

3. ENRICH YOUR FRENCH!

The following words tend to be overworked. To give one's French the necessary variety of language, they might well be replaced by one or other of their 'synonyms':

AIMER — adorer (*emphatic*); être passionné de, se passionner pour = to be very keen on (*objects*); être un fervent de = to be an enthusiast for (*e.g.*, *sports*); plaire à (*impersonal*)—*e.g.*, cette fleur lui plaît.

ALLER — rouler (*cars*); marcher (to function); naviguer (*ships*).

ALLER (à) — se rendre à (to make one's way to); s'approcher de (to come near); s'avancer vers (to go towards); se diriger vers (to make one's way towards).

AMI — le camarade; le compagnon (*tends merely to mean* a person you are doing something with); le copain (pal).

APPELÉ — intitulé (*books*); nommé.

APPORTER — amener (*person*).

APRÈS — ensuite (next); plus tard (later)—*adverbs*; *N.B.*—after he finished his task, he . . . , sa tâche finie, il...

AVOIR — posséder; être doué de (*natural faculties—e.g.*, *intelligence*); jouir de (to enjoy); être muni de (*equipped with something necessary—e.g.*, un passeport).

BEAUCOUP DE — bien des; de nombreux...; un grand nombre de; énormément de.

BON — fort (*e.g.*, fort en latin); sage (well-behaved).

COMME (like) — tel(le) que.

COMMENCER — entamer (*battle*, *conversation*, *etc.*); débuter (*intrans.*, to make a first appearance); commencer à = se mettre à.

DANS — dans le domaine de (*e.g.*, in literature, we find that . . .).

DEMEURER dans — habiter.

DIRE — déclarer, affirmer (*emphatic*); prétendre (to claim); annoncer; s'écrier (to exclaim); faire (*an interjection*).

ENTRER dans — pénétrer (*with some difficulty*) dans.

ÊTRE — se trouver (*position*, *place*); se montrer (to show oneself to be, prove to be).

FAIRE — construire (*rather laboriously—e.g.*, *a machine*); fabriquer (*in factory*); rendre (*before adjective*).

FINIR — (*trans.*) terminer, achever; (*intrans.*) cesser (*e.g.*, *noise*); se terminer (*an appointed end—e.g.*, *term*, *exam.*).

GARÇON — élève (*at school*); gamin (*on street*); gosse (lad, kid). Un garçon français = un jeune Français.

IL Y A — il existe (there is, there are, to be found); on trouve; se trouve(nt).

JEUNE FILLE — fillette (*small*); demoiselle (*young unmarried*); élève (*at school*); une jeune fille anglaise = une jeune Anglaise.

LIVRE — le volume; le tome—*e.g.*, dictionnaire en quatre tomes.

MAINTENANT — de nos jours (nowadays); à l'heure actuelle, actuellement (at the present moment).

PARTIR — s'en aller.

PENSER — croire (to believe); être d'avis (to be of the opinion); méditer, réfléchir; trouver, juger (to consider); songer (to dream, muse).

POUVOIR	savoir (to know how); être à même de (to be in a position to).
PRENDRE	enlever quelque chose à quelqu'un (to take away); saisir (une occasion) = to take an opportunity; tenir (*a house*, *a villa*); passer *(exam.)*. *N.B.*—il faut une heure pour arriver.
REGARDER	contempler (*fixedly*).
SAVOIR	apprendre (*a piece of news*); ne pas savoir = ignorer.
TRAVAIL	un œuvre (*e.g.*, de Molière); un effet—*e.g.*, la médecine a fait son effet; un emploi—*e.g.*, il est sans emploi; une tâche, une besogne (*specific job of work*).
TRAVAILLER	fonctionner, marcher (to function, go); labourer (to till).
TRÈS	bien, fort, extrêmement.
TROUVER	découvrir (to discover); rencontrer (to come across); apprendre (to find out).
VENIR	arriver; sortir (*e.g.*, d'une famille aristocratique); résulter (*e.g.*, qu'est-ce qui en résultera?); s'élever à (to come to, add up to); provenir de (to stem from).
VOIR	remarquer (to notice); apercevoir (to catch sight of); s'apercevoir de (to be aware of).
VOULOIR	désirer; avoir envie de; souhaiter (*in greetings*—*e.g.*, je vous souhaite un bon Noël).